HACK

CHICAGO VISIONS AND REVISIONS

*Edited by Carlo Rotella, Bill Savage, Carl Smith,
and Robert B. Stepto*

ALSO IN THE SERIES

The Third City: Chicago and American Urbanism
by Larry Bennett

The Wagon and Other Stories from the City
by Martin Preib

Soldier Field: A Stadium and Its City
by Liam T. A. Ford

Barrio: Photographs from Chicago's Pilsen and Little Village
by Paul D'Amato

*The Plan of Chicago: Daniel Burnham and
the Remaking of the American City*
by Carl Smith

DMITRY SAMAROV

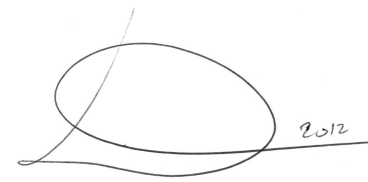

2012

HACK

STORIES FROM A CHICAGO CAB

The University of Chicago Press

Chicago and London

DMITRY SAMAROV WAS BORN IN THE SOVIET UNION AND IMMIGRATED TO THE
UNITED STATES IN 1978. HE EARNED HIS BFA IN PAINTING AND PRINTMAKING AT
THE SCHOOL OF THE ART INSTITUTE OF CHICAGO IN 1993 AND BEGAN DRIVING A CAB
THAT SAME YEAR. HIS WORK HAS BEEN SHOWN AT THE CHICAGO TOURISM CENTER,
THE MERCHANDISE MART, THE BOWERY GALLERY, AND BRANDEIS UNIVERSITY.
SAMAROV IS THE CREATOR OF THE BLOG *HACK*, STORIES FROM WHICH HAVE BEEN
FEATURED IN THE *CHICAGO READER* AND ELSEWHERE.

THE UNIVERSITY OF CHICAGO PRESS, CHICAGO 60637
THE UNIVERSITY OF CHICAGO PRESS, LTD., LONDON
© 2011 BY DMITRY SAMAROV
ALL RIGHTS RESERVED. PUBLISHED 2011.
PRINTED IN THE UNITED STATES OF AMERICA

20 19 18 17 16 15 14 13 12 11   1 2 3 4 5

ISBN-13: 978-0-226-73473-6 (CLOTH)
ISBN-10: 0-226-73473-0 (CLOTH)

SAMAROV, DMITRY, 1970–
    HACK STORIES FROM A CHICAGO CAB / DMITRY SAMAROV.
       P. CM. — (CHICAGO VISIONS AND REVISIONS)
    ISBN-13: 978-0-226-73473-6 (CLOTH: ALK. PAPER)
    ISBN-10: 0-226-73473-0 (CLOTH: ALK. PAPER)   1. TAXICAB INDUSTRY—
ILLINOIS—CHICAGO.   2. SAMAROV, DMITRY, 1970–   3. TAXICAB DRIVERS—
ILLINOIS—CHICAGO.   4. CHICAGO (ILL.)—SOCIAL LIFE AND CUSTOMS—21ST
CENTURY.   I. TITLE.   II. SERIES: CHICAGO VISIONS + REVISIONS.
    HD8039.T162U667 2011
    388.4'13214092—DC22   2011011322

♾ THIS PAPER MEETS THE REQUIREMENTS OF ANSI/NISO
Z39.48-1992 (PERMANENCE OF PAPER).

CONTENTS

PREFACE

In 1993 I graduated with a BFA in painting and printmaking from the School of the Art Institute of Chicago and moved back to Boston, where my family had settled in 1978 after leaving the Soviet Union.

I needed a job and, flipping through the want ads one day, saw a "Drivers Wanted" notice. It turned out to be from Checker Taxi of Boston. They told me where to take classes to obtain a Hackney Carriage License, and within two weeks I was behind the wheel of a hulking 1990 Chevrolet Caprice Classic, being told to go to Logan Airport by some jerk in a suit and having no idea how to get there.

I got the hang of it soon enough and kept at it for some three years. It paid my bills, allowed me to paint, and gave intimate access to the city and its inhabitants. Making pictures for me has always been about looking out the window at the surrounding world; being cloistered in an art-related field like teaching or illustration would have made the walls close in on me, whereas rolling around the streets provided ever-changing vistas. Sometimes it was ugly, sometimes beautiful. There was no need to invent or embroider because everything was out there to be seen; it was only a matter of putting in the time.

I moved back to Chicago in 1997 and ran through a succession of service industry jobs, continuing to paint all the while. Around 2000 I decided to attempt an illustrated book, or zine, about my Boston taxi-driving experiences. I called it *Hack* and, after spending innumerable hours at Kinko's, a first issue was printed in the spring of 2001. A second book followed about a year later, and that would have been that, except the day-job situation was becoming untenable. Anybody who has ever worked at a restaurant or bar knows that those places are vortices of bullshit drama and conflict. I've never been particularly good with authority figures; sooner or later there would always be a problem with some manager type. By 2003 I was frustrated enough to give cab driving another try. I revived *Hack* as a blog toward the end of 2006 in order to share some of what I'd seen.

Once again the city was open to me in the way that only this job allows. Cabdrivers catch people at the most revealing moments—not when they have their game faces on, but with their guard down, unable to pretend. To bear witness is both a privilege and a burden, but I don't regret getting back behind that wheel.

A Note about the Illustrations

Most of my pictures, for some twenty years, have been done while looking directly at the subject, so providing illustrations for these stories was a challenge. (I couldn't stop the car mid-fare and ask my passengers to pose for a drawing, could I?) Many of the pictures here were done from memory, and while creating them, I also would work out the wording of stories before actually typing them. Some are caricatures, some mere sketches, while some might even be their own finished visual statements. I used them as a break—that is, as an opportunity to try out different ways of constructing images. In any case, it was a way into the prose for a painter.

A Note about the Text

The blog from which this book was developed is organized chronologically, of course, whereas what follows is not. In searching for an organic structure that wasn't just a reprint of what had already been,

I settled on a days-of-the-week scheme—cab driving is a 24/7 industry, but some types of rides tend to happen earlier in the week, while
others will happen more toward the end. It's my hope that these
chapters will relate both the randomness and the order of my days
driving in the city.

GREETINGS

A raised hand generates an almost irresistible magnetic pull on a taxi driver. After some years, my mind is trained to seek its abstract form in light poles, reflections in parked cars, windblown tree branches, and, on a slow night, just about any likely shape into that desired signal—the symbol of time not spent in vain. Depending on the hour of day or night, what follows that hopeful gesture will vary from absolute silence to aggressive and often unwanted camaraderie, but in almost every case it begins with some sort of greeting.

On afternoons in the Loop, terse one- or two-phrase directives abound. Words like *Ogilvie, O'Hare, Wrigley, Lakeview, Bucktown, Midway, Michigan and Randolph, Ontario*, and *Chicago*, on and on. Like pushing the elevator button, they name their wish with no need for further communication. To expect more than an occasional *thank you* for the fare displayed on the meter and the sometime addition of a pre-calculated tip—worked out from countless identical trips— would be wishful thinking during downtown afternoons. There is a nonverbal contract made between passenger and driver to acknowl- edge that these transactions are basic and unremarkable, unworthy of excess comment or thought.

With the approach of twilight, tentative signals indicate that work mode is being shed and the thirst for social contact can be detected.

Between calls and texts, the passenger might ask about how the day's going, usually without expectation or need of any substantive response. Like exercise done at the gyms so many of them attend, this verbal stretch is meaningless except to keep limber in preparation for the heavier lifting that may lie ahead.

In early evening, couples wait at the curb, peering furtively at every passing taxi, sometimes raising their hands after the car has gone by, prompting slammed brakes from more aggressive or desperate drivers. A man wears his button-down untucked over nice jeans, his getup completed more often than not with flip-flops; his date is dressed to the nines from the 'do to the makeup to the little black dress to the heels that make her teeter long before her first cocktail. They'll exchange pleasantries in gratitude for the lift. He'll talk to the driver to show her he's got that common touch; she'll talk to the driver if she's bored with her guy or nervous. Once in a great while, there will be a conversation that reflects their good spirits, one that will serve to start off their date in a benevolent spirit toward all and sundry.

Packs of men pile in through the night. They'll start with: *Boss, Chief, Buddy, Dude, Man, Bro, Hey*, and when they think they're being funny, *Sir*. They've had a few or more by now, so they break the ice instinctively and without prompting. They'll ask how things have been, as if with a long-lost friend, and will even feign interest at the answer. They'll ask where the ladies are, then go back to recapping the "talent" encountered up to that moment. There's the possibility of inclusion in their club should I want in. A story or two about "those crazy bitches" could well qualify me for lifetime membership.

As taverns empty, the greeting runs the gamut from drunken mirth to stone silence. Tipsy chicks continue flirting in the cab as if still sipping appletinis. They laugh too loudly, say too much, and create more intimacy than there should be with a complete stranger. Some recount their evening if there's no one to dial up at this late hour, needing a confidant to vent to. They'll ask for advice or empathy with no regard for their listener's qualifications or character. Their need to ease their burden trumps the caution they might've displayed before the sun set. Last are the ones who were over-served and know it; with luck their address can be extracted without too much hassle, and they can be left to drift off into that end-of-the-night-ride-home fugue state. Upon arrival, the lights have to be raised and the drowsing reveler must be addressed in a loud voice: "HEY, BUDDY, PAL, CHIEF, TIME TO WAKE UP, YOU'RE HOME. TIME TO SAY GOOD NIGHT."

CAB LIFE

There are things that happen regularly to a cabdriver—the daily headaches at the garage; the tedious annual steps to renew a license; the constant run-ins with the same characters (whether fellow drivers or street people).

The forgettable details that add up to much of the time spent on this job.

At the Garage

This is the guy who owns the place. He thinks you're scum, and whatever you want, the answer's the same—"Fuck you."

If the cab breaks down, it's probably your fault, and *no*, you don't deserve any compensation for the time you lost. To save money, he imports retired cabs from New York and puts them on the street in Chicago. The fact that they break down every other week doesn't faze him in the least; in fact, it gives him an opportunity to scream at his mechanics or random other underlings to find out how they've wronged him. This is the quintessential angry little man; a miniature volcano ready to erupt at the slightest provocation. If you should happen to talk back, he'll accuse you of anger management issues and threaten to revoke your leasing privileges. Best to steer clear of him if you plan to stick around.

These are the people who relieve you of your money. They run the gamut from slow and stupid to unhinged and spiteful to friendly and efficient. It's a crap shoot—depending on whose line you get in, it can be a trying forty minutes or a breezy ten. Some will greet you politely, get through the lightening of your wallet, thank you, and send you on your way. Some will pick fights with drivers over unsigned credit card slips or other minor infractions; the screaming back and forth will make the rest in the queue more and more agitated until they start joining in. Others will yell for all to shut up, that the bickering is just holding the rest of us up. There'll be calm for a bit until a cashier starts moving too slow, a driver forgets to bring all required IDs to the window, or one doesn't like the look on the other's face; then the cacophony erupts once more.

All the cashiers snap to attention, however, when the angry little man walks in. They cower in his presence, and that gets them moving double-quick. When he's out of sight and earshot, they go back to their previous pace—be that frenetic or glacial.

Some of the drivers hang around the garage like house cats. I see the same ones puttering around, playing listless games of pool, or just pacing back and forth. They're not the ones waiting for their cab to get fixed or the ones hoping a cab becomes available; they park instead of driving and prefer the fumes from the body shop to those of the moving vehicles on the streets. How they make their living is a mystery.

A recurring drama plays out nearly every time there are more than three or four of us waiting in line to pay the leases on our taxis: a guy will get in line, stand for a minute or two, then wander off to chat with friends or use the bathroom. When he returns, inevitably the line has grown longer, and he'll attempt to convince the newcomers of his rightful place. Depending on their disposition and his approach, this seemingly simple situation can escalate into a hilarious screaming tirade, often resolved by a self-appointed elder statesman who takes it upon himself to explain the proper etiquette of the queue. The funny thing is that no one involved ever remembers the last time and is apt to repeat the performance when they come in the next day. Two grizzled old-timers get into it over the good old days—the first insists a medallion (a metal badge affixed to the vehicle's hood, which proves that it's licensed by the city to be a taxi-cab) costs 32K, the second dead sure they were 50K at the time in question. "He still smoking the cocaine, the old fool!" the burnout shouts to all within earshot as the object of his scorn walks away, the disagreement apparently settled. Standing and waiting is drudgery, and this little drama makes it all a little more worthwhile.

The drivers I spot in the garage are rarely encountered out in the city, but maybe they're unrecognizable when driving rather than fighting over their spot in line or bullshitting with their buddies. So much of it is context—stripped of their taxis, away from the streets, they're not the ones out there trying to hijack your fares, but just guys trying to get through the day.

Reeducation

Every year Chicago taxi drivers are made to renew their chauffeur's license. The requirements: getting a physical, which isn't much more than a blood pressure check and a $60 fee; peeing in a cup to screen for drugs; going to your cab company and getting a letter stating that you make the mandated effort to pick up radio calls in under-served areas; and, finally, going to the secretary of state for your driving record. This last item is what gets most of us because even one moving violation is cause to delay renewal of the license. And we all rack up more than one.

Driver Safety class is held in a windowless utility closet of a room on the mezzanine floor of the cab company's headquarters. Despite the 9 a.m. to 1 p.m. hours stated and underlined on the sign-up sheet, it doesn't really begin until 9:45. We spend half an hour taking attendance, then watch videos about car crashes and such. It's time for role-playing after that—one person is the driver and the other a passenger, and situations are reenacted to the laughter and guffaws of the peanut

gallery. A long, long lunch break kills two hours, then our instructor takes forty-five minutes to type up certificates proclaiming our successful completion of the course, and we're released to go back to work.

What is the purpose of this exercise? Perhaps it keeps city employees pushing paper or pixels. Yellow Cab doesn't charge its drivers a fee, but we can't get those hours back. Nothing is gained when time that could be spent earning a living is diverted to satisfy the whims of bureaucracy. Try driving eighty hours a week for a year and not getting a ticket—it's nearly impossible, so the city is assured of its repeat offenders annually.

The job is fraught with uncertainty, chaos, and danger, so it's a certain comfort to know that the city reserves a time for us every year to sit on our asses and bitch about our trials and tribulations. You'll see me there next year sitting in the back row doodling on the margins of the photocopied handouts to stay awake.

The Only White Cabdriver in Chicago

"You're the first white cabdriver I've ever had"—this, or some variant of it, is a common greeting when a customer enters the taxi. Sometimes "American" is substituted for "white," but in either case the implication is clear: *You're one of us, why on earth are you doing what we expect only our inferiors to be doing?* I usually congratulate them on their good fortune.

Either they want to hear my life story, or they want to launch into a litany of complaints about the "towelheads," the "sand niggers," the "slants," the "jigs," and all the other foreign strangers who cross their paths. Some want to bond over what they think unites us; this generally begins with sharing some bigoted remark aimed at other cabdrivers they've dealt with. When they don't receive a response, a pause follows, after which they say that they're not racist or anything, that they didn't mean to offend.

Two bruisers get in. They're headed to see the Blackhawks at the United Center and are a couple hours into their pregame preparations, to judge by the volume of their voices. "You're white."

I let it hang in the air, a strategy that gives the less brazen a chance to backtrack; not my passenger, who proceeds in a crude Hindi

accent to ape the ethnicity of his usual chauffeurs. His pal is greatly amused and gives some sort of African accent a go. At the stadium, they pause before paying to make sure I know that there's a few bucks extra to honor the pale shade of my skin. That's right, they gave me an $8 tip for being white.

Sometimes I feel compelled to explain that I wasn't born here, that English isn't my first language. This is usually met with disbelief. It's true that I've lived here a long time, and I pass for a native without much trouble. My family emigrated from the Soviet Union in 1978 when I was seven. While this was a long time ago now, no amount of time will make the immigrant's sense of being from elsewhere fade away.

Others broach the subject differently. "It's so great to have an American driver," a woman says. I ask what it is that thrills her about this, and she can't really put her finger on it. She assures me that she's no racist, then says she likes that I speak English. I tell her it's not my first language, and she's floored. Now it's suddenly fascinating to find out where people are from. There are *wow*s, *ooh*s, and *aah*s. She wears that appreciative smile that says she's learned something. Would she bother if I was wearing a turban and a full beard? A dashiki and cornrows?

Apparently even immigrants and minorities assume that a taxi driver is likely from the bottom of the barrel (or from a lower caste, color, or creed than whatever the passenger happens to be, at the very least). A black guy tells me that I'm not like most cabbies. "You know what I mean, man . . ."

"No, I don't," I answer.

An Indian student tells me that most drivers are Indian or Pakistani, and it shocks and confounds him to see me. "Why are you doing this?" he asks.

It's easier to condescend to a cabdriver if he has a thick accent, wears foreign garb, or can in any other way be thought of as lesser than oneself. Driving a cab is a first step for immigrants in this country. The education most gained in their home countries isn't recognized by our institutions, so they do what they have to, to put a roof over their heads. In that way I'm no different. Though my family came over when I was just a kid, in a sense I still haven't arrived here, and getting paid for what's important to me is but a pipedream. This is not to advocate for some color-blind, class-free utopia; having been born in one of those, I have no wish to return. Only a simple hope that new arrivals could be treated with a little more respect in a country founded by castoffs and mutts.

The Others

It's rare to run into a lifer who's happy about it. Most of them are burnouts, punch-drunk from breathing in exhaust for twenty, thirty years. One of the few I've met who is different is a guy named Ed. He loves to drive, has to do it every day. He owns his own cab, a Dodge Intrepid. We cross paths in our aimless treks around this town; sometimes I see him with his old lady at the Music Box Theatre.

Last night one of the oldsters sat at a green light ahead of me. After waiting a reasonable few seconds, I tried to maneuver around to his right. He rolled down the passenger-side window and started screaming. Neither my customers nor I could figure out his problem, to be so obviously wrong yet act with such righteous rage. The confrontation ended with him being forced to brake after I very intentionally cut him off; sometimes a point has to be made.

Most drivers aren't that far gone. They chatter to each other on their cells, argue loudly at the airport, race one another down Michigan Avenue. There are occasional feeble attempts to unionize, to band together against the powers that be: the city, the cab company, the customers, the wives. All these efforts are likely doomed to failure because the job is for lone wolves, and part-time ones at that. We're all aspiring to be elsewhere, and like the fares who slam the door behind them as they exit, most of us want out in the worst way.

Burnout

I saw him in the left turn lane on LaSalle the other day, waiting to go west on Chicago. He rolled down the window and yelled out a question to a couple walking past. Obviously dumbfounded, they kept walking as if the cabbie had never engaged them in any way, while he smiled to himself, continuing the conversation under his breath.

I used to see him at the Checker garage before it went out of business and was absorbed by Yellow Cab. A worn puffy winter coat with a hood, thick black glasses, a black shirt with the top button buttoned and dandruff dotting his chest like a light dusting of snow on a winter's eve, white hair groomed in a '50s sort of way, buzzed short around the ears and neck. His skin reddened to an unhealthy hue, though probably not from boozing; he doesn't seem like the type—

though what do we ever really know about people when they're out of our sight? He'd be in line to pay the lease on his cab, trying to shoot the shit with the others, coming off like some sort of space alien, causing them to take a step or two back, as if the distance would keep his insanity from crawling up their legs.

His name is Mike—his last name escapes me. He's been a taxi driver a long, long time. He's got a collection of plastic garbage bags that he hauls around like luggage; the big black one has a note written in thick marker taped to it. I've never been able to make out what it says, though it starts with his name and goes on to cover most of the side of the bag. When he's waiting at the long table in the drivers' room, it's his pillow when he's passed out.

He'll only drive a Checker when most of the fleet are Yellow cabs—this means that he'll wait many hours longer more often than not. No incoming driver escapes his interrogations: "You dropping?

Is it a Checker? No . . . Oh, all right." Many drivers back up or take the long way in an attempt to evade his attentions. Save for once telling him to get the hell away from me when he stood too close in line, I'd almost avoided any substantive interaction with him over the years. But one time we'd both been at the garage for hours, and on one of my strolls outside, he cornered me. He talked about his loneliness, of his landlady raising his rent; he asked if I had family, saying he had none. There was no graceful way to disengage, short of just walking away. So that's what I did.

He's the walking embodiment of our worst fears—a solitary, forgotten man twisted and broken by a job that tests the endurance of those much better equipped than he ever could've been. He's what we end up as in our nightmares: barely tolerated in this world, just enough to be able to draw breath.

Blessed

He haunts the taxi barn. He stows his belongings behind the enclosure where new cars are spray-painted into cabs—coats, lawn chairs, and other discarded treasures arranged to approximate a living room of sorts. His head pops up to greet drivers slinking in to pay their lease or argue about the disrepair of the vehicles that the shop has foisted on them. Other times he's outside earning a few bucks, wiping down the cars fresh from the wash. He's scarecrow-thin and wears his Kangol backward over a stocking cap.

I leave cigarettes for him next to a boom box that blares R&B. "He wanted me to wash his personal car, and the water froze as soon as it hit the hood, no point in it. Why even bother in this shit?" he wonders aloud. When asked about how he's doing, he always says he's blessed. "Cuz I don't worry, no use to. I seen 'em die doin' this job. Know why? They worry and it kills 'em. They say, 'You're homeless, you got nothin', how do you get by?' and I tell 'em that the Lord'll take care of me."

He shares his Bugler tobacco if I'm out and compliments my easygoing disposition. A few remaining teeth show in the smile that doesn't spread to his eyes. "You smoking today?" he asks, knowing that the answer is almost always yes.

He knows not to ask for money but for rides instead. He usually goes to the gas station at the edge of what's left of the Cabrini-Green housing projects. "Gotta get me some food—give me a lift?" He has me drop him across the street so as not to be seen getting out of the cab; don't want to seem like you've got more than you do—in case someone's watching. One time he said he was going to see a woman he had up in the high-rise. "Only way to get warm," he said. "I'm blessed."

Queues

We spend hours waiting: hundreds of Crown Vics, Intrepids, Scions, and minivans of various make line up at O'Hare and Midway air-

ports, queuing to be dispatched out to the terminals. Time is passed wiping the winter grime off quarter panels and windshields with soiled newspaper from overflowing trash barrels, wetted by spray bottles or graying slush. Clusters of drivers commiserate about lousy tips and inconsiderate passengers, about overzealous cops and clueless airport workers. The politics of a couple dozen countries is dissected, debated, and argued over again and again. Accented English in every variety as well as some hundred foreign tongues clash then disperse into the frigid winter air.

We walk up and down the rows and rows of cabs for exercise; we go to the restaurant and buy food and then loiter around the counter talking to buddies, blocking the way of others trying to put their orders in; we buy porn DVDs from the guys walking around hawking all matter of useless wares; we pray to Allah in a strange glassed-in area provided for that purpose; we gather in backseats, fogging the windows with our words, peering out occasionally to check on the glacial flow of lanes; we hope for that home run, the fare that makes up for all these hours lost, for the daily dry spells that test even the hardest of veterans; we stare at the hundreds of vehicles around us and wonder why such an awesome fleet assembled for conveyance makes us feel like we're going nowhere, or maybe we sit and hope the next fare will be our last.

No matter how long it's been though, every lane will have that one cab that stands mute and inert when the time to move comes. The driver's asleep in the backseat, using the bathroom, or across the lot obliviously solving the worries of the world. The chorus of horns is quickly followed by a parade of detouring vehicles, artfully dodging the loping dawdler, who desperately sprints back to his suddenly lonesome-looking taxi.

Back in the city, every hotel and office building hosts its own collection of idlers, all hoping to go back to the airport. Lunch trucks dish out African meals as the cabs inch slowly toward the entrance, and panhandlers walk up and down, greeting each new arrival with the same futile request. The doorman hauling luggage inspires an extra-eager pump of the gas pedal, followed by a jolting stop, inches from the quarry.

During off-hours, the car washes attract hordes, every few drivers struggling to negotiate the runners leading inside, tires slipping, sending the car rocking back and forth until the course is righted. Homeless men wait on the other side, hoping to earn a few bucks wiping the excess freezing droplets off the dripping taxis.

At any time of day, the cashiers at the garage take money for the privilege of sitting behind the wheel for another twenty-four hours. At the window, the litany of excuses is never-ending. There's always a very good reason why we shouldn't pay the late fees, why we haven't paid for three days and shouldn't be expected to. When we're informed of the amount due, there's a mad search through pockets, socks, and satchels for crumpled bills; as if the preceding half hour of standing around couldn't possibly have prepared us for this unexpected development. The price of the lease seems to blindside us; a novel and heretofore unforeseen hardship. As the rest—our money ready in hand—groan and wince, the wronged man continues to plead his case, then leaves, either with eyes averted or defiant and unbowed.

Outside, we navigate past haphazardly parked comrades, in and out of potholes and rutted blacktop, back onto the thoroughfares of the city. We search for spots to linger, the spots that lead us to far-off places, to that one place where the driver's door can be closed behind us, not to be opened again.

Relief

One of the few true hardships of driving a taxi is that there's no bathroom provided in the office. This makes one a crack detective and true connoisseur of public facilities—from the lowliest shitter to the most well-appointed powder room.

The men's room at the O'Hare Airport taxi staging area may perhaps represent the most extreme test for the driver with a full bladder. Used by thousands of malodorous unhappy men each day, there's just no way the custodial staff could possibly keep up even if they wanted to. The reek at times attains a physical shape and force such that to merely hold one's breath is of little use. Besides that, the place seems to function like a drawing room or parlor to some—conversations continue stall to stall and side by side at the urinal trough. Those waiting to use the stalls stand sentry between the sinks and entrance, often requiring deft circumnavigation in order to shorten one's own stay.

A steady stream of pigeon-toed cabbies pours into the side entrance at the Hyatt Regency on Wacker. The combination of easy access and availability of temporary parking in the hotel's cab line makes this one of the premium stops downtown. Rushing past lolling guests and employees is quick and easy, and one can be back on the road in no time. The only downside is the traffic we must vanquish in order to reach this little oasis; this, of course, will make eventual arrival that much more hard-won. When the ladies at the coffee kiosk in the lobby compliment you on your haircut, you know you've been a cabbie for a good long time.

Fox & Obel offers a worthy alternative, though the fifteen-minute standing zone can hold no more than five vehicles at a time. Fox & Obel is a gourmet market catering to the privileged, so the latrines are kept spic-and-span, which is much appreciated by the weary driver. Overpaying for a cup of coffee while in the company of the moneyed class is an added bonus.

Dunkin' Donuts dot the city and attract hacks as well as cops, bums, and drunken revelers at all hours. The bathroom locks here vary according to the whims of the franchisees that oversee these establishments. From buzzer systems operated from behind the counter, to keys attached to worn chunks of wood or plastic that must be passed from user to user in an awkward, stuttering relay race, to plain old first-come, first-serve—depending on one's level of need, these obstacles can be tackled with greater or lesser good humor and equanimity.

Gas stations are beacons. However, their welcoming neon glow is sometimes fool's gold. From the dubious "Out of Order" signs that mysteriously appear as the sun sets, to reticent security personnel who take the request to unlock the loo as a personal affront, the simple journey to empty one's bladder or bowels may be fraught with unnecessary and unforeseen detours. On the flip side, some friendly and understanding clerks don't give a second look to the desperately hustling men dashing past aisles of candy, if said men are regular paying customers.

An awareness of port-o-potties located just off the highway can be the difference between a pleasant afternoon and dire embarrassment. There are times sitting in gridlock with a fare in tow that my prayers have been known to be addressed to Jesus, Allah, Yahweh, and any other relevant authority for safe and unsullied passage to our destination. Passengers have related stories of other cabbies using bottles and jars kept for just such emergencies. Perhaps it's my Eastern European upbringing, but that's a bridge I have yet to cross. When worst comes to worst, an alley or abandoned lot and an open cab door or two provides sufficient shelter to take care of impending emergencies.

All in all, no matter our supposed sophistication, this daily reminder of our physical ties to the natural world serves to put even the mightiest among us on equal footing. We're all just animals looking for a little relief.

Five Percent

"You take credit, right?" the girl stumbling from the bar asks apologetically. Hearing a *yes*, she exhales, relaxes, and tells of the many times that the answer was *no*. The fact that I've made this exception for her by allowing payment with plastic makes me the "Best Cabdriver Ever!" in her eyes. She's not alone, but merely the latest of many riders overjoyed to take advantage for the first time of an option that's been mandated for some five or six years—the city requires every taxi in Chicago to accept credit cards.

When the credit card rules were instituted, the cab companies saw an easy way to cash in—they slapped an extra 2 to 3 percent on top of the usual processing fees, diverting a steady trickle their way on every single transaction. That 5 percent is what's made the equipment in many a taxi suddenly cease to function at the prospect of plastic; the flustered customer, not knowing any better, agrees to the detour to the ATM that the driver helpfully suggests, and everyone's left with a sour taste in their mouths. Most cabbies don't want to lie, but the guarantee of losing some crumbs from the precious scrap they've worked so hard to snare is more than they can stomach; the passenger feels like he was taken advantage of or treated rudely at minimum, when all that any hack wants is to be paid what he's owed.

Aside from yammering on cell phones and not being "American," this has been the top complaint I hear about other cabdrivers for as long as I can remember. It puts me in the unenviable position of rat-

ting out colleagues while also losing precious pennies, all to appear
aboveboard. It's not much of a victory having to inform a customer
that the way to make the card swipe in other taxis magically function
again is to threaten a call to Consumer Services. The sad fact is that
none of us are in much of a position to take a stand, so when drivers
refuse to accept credit, it only makes the rest of us look bad.

Touch screens have started appearing in our town. The local cab
companies imported these backseat credit card systems from New
York. The stated aim is to allow better customer service, but the real
purpose is to squeeze out a few extra coins at the expense of the drivers' fraying nerves. The ads and programming haven't yet begun,
but they're just around the corner. This was confirmed when I had
to take a cab with a malfunctioning screen in to the shop. There was
a creepy industrial hiss on a constant loop escaping from the speaker.
While this would've been a fitting soundtrack to a David Lynch film,
two weeks' worth of it was driving the unsuspecting public a little insane. The mechanic got rid of it by yanking one of the wires wedged
between the front seats and the partition; but soon the humming and
wheezing will be replaced by commercials, and many of us will be
taking a hammer to those screens if there isn't a mute button.

For now, a silent slide show of Chicago boosterism must suffice for entertainment. Shots of the Art Institute, the lakefront, and the skyline with the unbuilt Chicago Spire flash past those not too bleary-eyed to take note. Many late-night debates have ensued from the architectural rendering of that ill-fated corkscrew tower. "Where the HELL is that supposed to be? That isn't here . . ." is the consensus. Otherwise, upon spying the flickering images, they'll declare, "Oh cool, you got a TV back here, bro! Got porn?"

Lost Souls

Making countless passes up and down the thoroughfares, we begin to seek out landmarks as a way of reconfirming our own place in the city. Some of them turn out not to be prominent structures, but human characters that make an area their own through persistence and stubborn refusal to fade away. Most of them wouldn't exactly be considered pillars of the community. In fact, they aren't part of any block club, yet their presence marks the mental image of the locale they haunt more than any neighborhood booster ever could.

The double-amputee at Dearborn and Congress waits patiently for the light to go red before wheeling up to the stopped vehicles, looking for alms. He's been here for years and doesn't hurry. He seems to know the precise second to hit the sidewalk to avoid injury and dirty looks.

From the Magnificent Mile to Wacker Drive, a regular visitor will spot him sooner or later. He's got brushed long gray hair and clothes that hang off him in that coat-hanger way, as if to prove that they were given to him rather than chosen. From a distance, he looks a bit like Daniel Day-Lewis, with the prominent nose and deep-set eyes; up close, the blotchy skin and bad teeth don't seem like any movie star's. He isn't dirty, and his clothes, while not his own, are always clean, and I've never seen him ask for money or much of anything. Mostly, he fills his days crossing and re-crossing major downtown streets. It's as if he's been put out there to wander, cleaned up and re-dressed overnight, then told to do it again and again and again.

She's made Chicago and Western hers. Any of the bus shelters or

benches in the vicinity are liable to hold her bundle of bags and rags. Her hair is dreaded into one ugly gray-brown clump to the side of her bent-over head as she makes her way slowly down the sidewalk. The object is to transport one or another of the many pieces of her self-styled luggage from one spot to the next. Sometimes it's all gathered together to board the #49 or #66 bus, to the great annoyance of the CTA drivers and passengers; the operation takes many minutes, and she's years past caring about any kind of recrimination. The picking up and putting down of all those worthless bits is just another way to bide away the time until the sand in the hourglass runs out.

She patrols the six-way intersection of Damen, Fullerton, and Elston. Walleyed and slight, she staggers toward cars, holding out an oversize plastic cup. Her mouth hangs open and to the side at an unnatural cant, and the sounds she makes can't truly be classified as words. It's customary to make oneself pitiful to elicit sympathy and remuneration, but she takes it to an absurd extreme, if indeed it's any of her own doing. That face wouldn't be out of place in one of Hieronymus Bosch's tableaux of hell. Her occasional replacement is a black man whose limbs all move the wrong way as he walks; a worthy substitute to play her part on that stage.

These people, and many others less memorable, serve as signposts all across this town. There's some kinship between them and the hacks who haunt these avenues; these forgotten shades serve as the only constant company on deserted streets at any hour of the day or night. Their presence reaffirms our own, while also reminding us of the merciless repetition of this work. Like them, we must return again and again to the same intersections, with luck to get just enough fortune for the chance to do it all over once more.

MONDAY

Monday is a day to pick up a cab if you don't have one, or to get the one you have serviced. Odds are that what a driver makes this day will just cover the cab lease and get him closer to the more lucrative days of the week.

There are long fallow periods—hours spent just wandering—and the occasional passengers that do appear are often odd or off; strange types that we sometimes wish would have just stayed home.

Eighteen Hours

2:42 A.M.

I arrive at the garage, look at the waiting list for cabs, put in my chauffeur's number: fifth on the list. I settle in with my back against the Ms. Pac-Man machine and start a drawing.

4:08 A.M.

The drawing's done after a smoke break and some aimless ambling to and fro. Other drivers take turns sauntering up to the list, scanning hopefully for some progress, though the cashier hasn't laid a hand on it yet. The empty time inspires a kind of magical thinking, where it's possible to convince ourselves that subtle signs invisible to others have significance.

5:02 A.M.

The whole time, every few minutes, drivers come in and stride purposefully toward the window. We all zero in, searching for the meter in hand; this would mean he might be dropping his car, thereby paving the path for our release. The ones who do turn in meters are all putting their cabs in the service line, meaning that they have breakdowns and their names will be put at the front of the waiting list, ahead of us.

5:47 A.M.

The overnight skeleton crew washes, waxes, buffs, and otherwise attends to the half dozen cars headed for City Inspection in the morning. If they pass, there's a chance that they may be dispatched, though this prospect is hours away at best. It's something to hold on to, a wisp of a chance to make the time feel worthwhile.

6:00 A.M.

A flurry of activity. The morning garage crew comes in, followed by the morning manager and the boss, who casts his jaundiced eye around the place before disappearing into the office. The lifts and other machinery spring to life to provide a soundtrack of grinding, hissing violence that tests our fraying, taciturn dispositions. Three cabs are assigned, though with all the accumulated breakdowns, the list is now longer than it was three hours ago.

7:53 A.M.

A walk outside reveals the high merciless sun, which feels no sympathy for those of us who've endured this sleepless night. The overnight cashier is relieved by three morning ones, all windows now ready to receive lease money and endure complaints and hard-luck stories. Those who protest vociferously enough are directed around the corner, through the manager's office door, where their concerns are mostly ridiculed and ignored before they are dismissed and sent on their way. Periodically, one or another approaches to ask how long the wait has been, to sympathize or share their own troubles, making it all the more excruciating because the best we can do here is cast our minds elsewhere, to have an imaginary reprieve.

11:01 A.M.

Lunch break for the day shift. The roach coach pulls in to dispense coffee, candy, pop, tacos, and a Cuban sandwich so ancient it may've predated the Castro regime. The waiting-room table—previously cluttered with half-read newspapers, books, and the crossed arms of nappers—is now further littered with wrappers, crumbs, and empty Coke cans. A man with a work shirt monogrammed with the name *Jose* pushes piles of dust and detritus around with an old broom before collecting it into a dustpan and dragging it gradually toward a Dumpster.

1:33 P.M.

ID numbers are called out, inspiring a rush toward the window whether the numbers match our own or not, the cashier telling the stragglers to sit back down; those not present when their turn is called are crossed off the list, those just arriving informed that no more will be taken this day. Some loiter around anyway, chewing the fat with their buddies or playing halfhearted games of pool, punctuated by loud disputes about the true rules of the game. When the list is taken down, we brace anxiously for some bit of progress, studying the worn sheet of crossed-out and newly added digits, as it's returned to its place next to the row of cashiers' windows.

3:53 P.M.

My attempt to purchase Munchos from the vending machine is temporarily thwarted as the bag lodges horizontally aloft above the door slot, refusing to drop any farther. Banging and shaking doesn't do a thing, neither does the purchase of Bacon & Cheddar Potato Skins, bought in the hope of jarring it loose with their own fall. Another driver saves the day by getting his own Munchos. "Problem solved!" he states proudly. I smoke the last of my American Spirits in the unshaded glare of the afternoon. Trips to the washroom to throw water at my face only serve to emphasize the extent of sleep deprivation.

The office is now darkened, the higher-ups' day done, but the parade of payers rarely slackens; they jostle each other, feigning outrage as they squeeze toward the slots that relieve them of their earnings. I've tried every possible place to sit, lean, or slump over. What's left, more often than not, is a dazed and wavering stance with eyes unfocused; a zombie-like existence that feels as if it has neither beginning nor end.

8:37 P.M.

A beckoning finger draws me toward the window, followed by the clink of a car key hitting the metal basin of the slot. With the fee for the remaining hours of the evening collected, I'm free to go forth and seek my fortune. Eighteen hours at the garage, thirty-three since I last slept, lucky not to have driven into a light pole on my way home; dead to the world before head hits pillow.

Bus, Bike, Walk

If cars are the fish, then city buses are the whales in the water of the thoroughfare. Slow, lumbering, and able to go where and when they want, they put the rest of us in our place simply by their girth. During rush hour, they mass in the right lane to form an impenetrable wall; God help the lowly sedan hoping to make a right turn. When these behemoths are ready to stir, they'll take up two to three lanes

to make their move, causing an absolute stop behind them while the road ahead is all clear. The worst offenders are the accordion buses, which hamper passage like nothing else on wheels. A few weeks ago, one overshot its stop, then turned its front half toward the curb to block both lanes while disgorging its contents. When it eventually pulled forward, I went around and slammed on the brakes, making him halt, to communicate my displeasure. The irate bus driver threw it into park at the next red light, ran up to my passenger-side window screaming bloody murder, turning an unflattering crimson shade that made me fear for his health. The gist of the rant was that he'd had it with cabdrivers getting in his way and flouting the rules of the road; laughable considering the mismatch in size and potential for damage and distress between the two vehicles. All the same, any

opportunity to cause a CTA bus a bit of annoyance can't be passed over by any self-respecting taxi driver.

Lower on the food chain, but presenting their own special problems, are the cyclists. The regular riders downtown often seem hell-bent to squeeze through any available inch between vehicles while simultaneously giving only cursory attention to streetlights and stop signs. Bike couriers, of course, elevate this dance to an art form. A while back, one of them wrote a memoir comparing their vocation to that of ninjas, medieval knights, and other mythical warriors; nothing like self-delusion to get one through the drudgeries of the day. As a lowly fellow servant to the moneyed class, hearing such claptrap mixes funny with sad. Last week one of them yelled, "YOU'RE A DOUCHE!" as she took exception to a U-turn I'd made, which, coming as it did within thirty feet of her precious fixed-gear steed, apparently presented some grievous threat. Pulling even and telling her that it takes one to know one got a half-smile out of her; we hopscotched back and forth for at least two miles down Damen, with more chatter and gesticulating. If it wasn't quite understanding, it was at least détente.

Pedestrians are the frailest yet most dangerous creatures of the road; the gentlest nudge with the bumper may mean the end of one's workday, not to mention the time-consuming cleanup. At times it takes heroic self-control not to mow down a dozen or two just on general principle. When the quitting bell rings, they swarm the sidewalks, often spilling over into the roadways. They cast dirty looks at motorists who deign to remind them to retreat back to their part of the street, then test brakes by not breaking pace no matter the shade of the traffic signal. Some fancy themselves amateur crossing guards, windmilling their arms at moments of their choosing, further enraging many a veteran wheelman.

These little run-ins are an ideal way to relieve the frustrations of the day; we can sense when the driver, the cyclist, or the pedestrian is poised on that precipice—ready to explode at the slightest provocation. After a time, it can become a sort of game to set them off, if not a source of pride at least; a method to soothe one's own rapidly fraying nerves.

White Eagle

I am first in line outside McCormick Place to pick up the hordes leaving the Chicago Auto Show and watch as she teeters toward the cab on her frail birdlike legs. Her destination is the nearest bar, which she croaks slurring, sounding more drugged than drunk. Outside a tavern some five blocks away, told that I wouldn't be joining her inside, she instructs me to take her to Naperville.

What does she look like? Well, if Britney Spears makes it to her late sixties, or maybe even her early fifties with enough abuse, that

would be her. Black leggings and top, bleached-blond hair, and enough makeup to make a corpse pomaded by an undertaker look tasteful by comparison.

The ride through rush-hour traffic mostly passes with her drifting in and out of consciousness, wondering if we are there yet, and yammering in a surprisingly coherent tone on her cell. In downtown Naperville, she asks to stop at a tavern and for me to wait. A half hour passes as the meter ticks on and on. Finally, I go inside to find her slumped over, muttering to her neighbors at adjoining bar stools. They help her out to the cab, and we pull out. It's not long before she tells me that she doesn't know where she is. When this happens in the city, it's not a problem because it's laid out in a grid, so one's got to really try to get lost; the suburbs are another story, between the winding roads, endless trees, and countless interchangeable strip malls.

The only clue I have are the words "White Eagle," which she intones any time I ask again where she lives. We meander about, unable to find that secret locale for another twenty minutes before my third attempt to get directions from a White Hen Pantry finally pays off. It turns out to be a golf course/country club/gated community kind of place. She pays and staggers toward a well-lit house as if nothing out of the ordinary has occurred.

Oyster Crackers

It's pouring and the crutches soften my heart enough to stop. He gets on his cell and says, "Damn, baby! All's I wanted was some

oyster crackers . . . You know I cain't have no chili without 'em . . . You couldn't do that one thing fo' me . . . ."

He hangs up and explains that his lady has made chili, but all her cooking is bland like school cafeteria food. He needs some flavor in his chili, some hot sauce and oyster crackers. Now she wants her son, who's no kid (he's eighteen; she's thirty-five), to go to the store. "I got a married bitch too," he says. "That blew my mind . . . men cheat because they can, women because they want to . . . ."

Having shared his wisdom, he hobbles out to spice up his bland chili.

A Smoker

She pulls the rolling suitcase wearily toward the top of the cab line at Terminal 3, leaves it by my trunk without so much as a word, and gets into the backseat. "Marriott Downtown," she says, breaking away from her phone conversation momentarily, then resuming

it in a voice so loud that I can't help but overhear. We melt into the inbound Monday-afternoon traffic from O'Hare with her words providing the soundtrack. The subject seems to be someone close to her and his inability to manage his finances. Checks bounce and a new strategy has to be devised so that life can be led more responsibly. "My phone's about to die. I'll call you when I get to the hotel room. Love you," she finishes, hanging up and turning her attention my way.

The flight had been turbulent. So much so that she'd had to go into the airport bathroom to re-iron her hair. "What I need now is for you to stop somewhere so I can buy me some cigarettes. I don't really smoke. I'm a doctor too, not a medical one, a psychologist. Even Obama's gotta hide it . . . Me and my best friend had a deal— we'd share one pack a month, but since she got divorced, she doesn't need to keep it from her husband and has as many as she wants. Anyways, they're at her house. Know how hard it is for us in California? We have to creep around behind everyone's back." I tell her that I know that need too well. Having kicked the habit after almost twenty years, there is no way I'll stand in the way of anyone needing to scratch that itch.

"It has to be a particular brand and a certain time of day for me," she explains, as we pull off the Kennedy at Irving Park and turn into a Shell station.

She emerges with a pack of Benson & Hedges 100s and a purple Bic. I tell her she's welcome to smoke in the cab, but she prefers to indulge out on the curb just to the side of the store's doors.

"I'd have to crack the window, and my hair would be ruined again. Anyway, I don't want you to watch me sin. Please look away." She lights up, and a quarter of the cigarette's length turns to ash with the first hungry inhale. Her straightened black hair looks like it is just barely holding on, stray strands rebelling against the ironing and product and sticking out from the hardened shape of the rest.

"Feel *so* much better now," she announces, getting back in. "Never used to smoke until I had kids, then everything went to hell. You know, they don't tell you this, but they get to be teenagers and they become assholes." She wants to know if having a cigarette every once in a while makes her a smoker, and I answer that to me it's like being a little bit pregnant—that is, if you smoke, then you're a smoker. This doesn't please her but does make her laugh.

Her craving satisfied, she wants to know how the shopping is near her hotel. She's pleased to be deposited in the middle of the Magnificent Mile, where one can max out a charge card in minutes with very little effort. Maneuvering into the Marriott's narrow drive on Rush Street, I run her credit card, then pop out to help with her luggage, but the doorman has already gotten it and she's some ten feet away, hiding behind one of the columns to light up again.

Demons

I'm stopped at a red at Chicago and State just past the YMCA on a blustery evening when a guy bolts across the street and gets in through the left rear door of the cab without any warning.

"Take me to 79th and Halsted . . . No, better take me to the 35th Street Po-lice Station, my sister's there."

We head southbound on Lake Shore Drive, and he asks, "What is this? Lake Shore? . . . Oh, OK . . ." Just then a hulking SUV's headlights overtake us, and he jerks his head around, then ducks out of view as if under the hail of enemy fire.

"Who's that? Don't know why they're tryin' ta kill me. Somethin' that happened to one of the other guys at the place I was stayin', now they're after me . . . Have ya heard about it?"

A few moments of silence is broken by his sudden suspicion that we've passed our exit, a tone that implies complicity in the conspiracy against him; after I reassure him by pointing out roadside landmarks to verify our course, he apologizes but remains vigilant.

We pull up, and he hands over a money clip as collateral. "Gotta go inside to get the rest," he explains, and runs into the overlit lobby of the police station. An inventory of the clip yields four singles, a Link Card (electronic food stamps), a library card, and a state ID all miraculously under the same name with a picture that even bears some resemblance to my passenger.

He returns with a uniformed woman—couldn't say if she was a cop or a security guard—who leans through the window and asks how much he owes. "Ain't got that much, gotta go back upstairs for my wallet, all right?" she says, then asks him where he's spending the night, and when he tells her, she hollers, "Stanley, ain't got no damn cell to put ya in!" Nevertheless, he gathers his things from the backseat and slinks toward the glass doors . . .

Ten minutes later she's back, and upon hearing about the forces fomenting the man's demise can only shake her head wearily; the demons are no stranger to her. She overtips and tells me to be safe, then shivers and pulls her coat close against the windswept night.

Gangway

Late one night, the dispatcher directs me to an address off Fullerton near Logan Square. I pull up and a woman with ratty bleached-blond hair and a tie-dyed shirt comes out carrying a bunch of plastic bags. Placing the load in the backseat, she gives an *Oh well* kind of look and shrugs before shivering against the chill and retreating back toward the house. A heavily made-up Latina is next out. She seems more intent on her phone conversation than actually making it from the doorway to the cab, but gradually that gap narrows, then closes.

"Forty-third and Western, you can take the highway," she directs before lapsing into silence. Her curly hair shines slick with oily product, her lipstick applied and reapplied generously to form a sort of patina, enough mascara to cause a raccoon envy, and various other tinctures to alter or hide the true nature of her visage. She has those long acrylic nails, the ones encrusted with fake diamonds. The parts that are unadorned are a Day-Glo teal.

As we speed past downtown, she quietly intones into her cell, "C'mon, baby, I know you can do it. I believe in you, you make me so proud . . . You the MAN, don't be a negative, baby . . . just the way we talked about, I love you *sooo* much."

We get off the Stevenson, and she directs me up Archer toward Western. McKinley Park is dead-still at this hour. As with most neighborhoods in the city, 1 a.m. on a Monday is a time to quietly gird for the coming workweek. We speed down the avenues, unchecked by other vehicles, hardly slowed by traffic lights, before coming to rest on a narrow one-way street in front of a neatly appointed single-family abode. She hurriedly rechecks her makeup in the mirror. ". . . so tired," she murmurs under her breath while counting out the price of the fare.

"Do I look OK?" she asks, making eye contact for the first time, revealing the faint, mostly healed bruise on her left cheek. She gathers up her belongings and drags them to the black metal gangway gate on the side of the house. She asks me to stay until she's made it inside, so I sit there watching her fumble with the lock. The motion detector lights and darkens the porch every other minute. Giving up, she comes back to the cab. "My key won't work, I need to call my fiancé to come out and unlock it. Don't leave, please." She argues her case into the cell for what seems like eons before a guy in a hoodie and shorts appears and grudgingly unlocks the gate. They disappear between the two houses without looking back.

Vampire Hours

Hauling up and down empty avenues on winter weeknights can be its own kind of purgatory. But at those instances when one feels like the last being drawing breath, the others make their presence felt. The truly dedicated drinkers, the lonely lunatics for whom time of day or place don't matter, the speed-addled tow truckers, the cops looking for an excuse, and the other cabbies fool enough to be out fighting over the few sorry scraps left to be had.

The winter snow-route parking ban brings schools of haulers out onto the quiet thoroughfares to conduct their insane death races. Tow trucks turn feral at night, treating moving vehicles like stationary obstacles, paying only cursory attention to traffic signals, ignoring lane configurations altogether. To have one of these panting, hungry beasts riding your ass will wake you from the deepest reverie. Dragging carcasses back to the yard doesn't slow their pace any; some leave a trail of sparks off some poor SUV's bumper in their wake, no time for niceties in their feeding frenzy. Like taxis, each is adorned with its own war paint or coat of arms, and each seems dimly aware of the competition without allowing for any more than tense tolerance. They're lone wolves by nature, out to get their prey, to stash it, then come back for more.

The cops sit in their cruisers, driver's side to driver's side, talking about whatever it is that cops talk about. The blue swirling lights, visible for miles, cause the rest of us to approach with trepidation, then veer slowly into oncoming lanes to avoid them, cursing under our breath about tax dollars, double standards, and all those other things we can't or won't ever change. Other cops fly by, sirens blaring, en route to back up their brethren, five or six of them surrounding some souped-up Toyota with after-market rims, spinners, maybe some neon. Several usually guard the perimeter, making sure their rites aren't scrutinized too closely by the laity. Best to keep one's head down and glide by meekly, away from any chance to rouse their suspicions.

The odd types who'll venture out on these nights when they should really stay in just don't know any better. The ones who aren't on urgent missions to or from their local tavern want things that never quite add up. The cheerful, ragged girl from Ukrainian Village is one. She wants to go to the West Side. Then she asks to stop at Village Pizza on Chicago and Western for a slice, when we'd already passed it. Next, she insists on going by the place with the bullet-proof glass for her smokes. Then the CITGO station after that, where she runs in with her cigarette still half-lit, spending a good five minutes inside as the meter ticks away and emerging with a fistful of lottery tickets and a box of Boo Berry cereal.

"Never see this shit anymore, couldn't help gettin' it. These motherfuckers out here don't realize I got a taxi waiting. They take they sweet-ass time . . ." She has me drop her at an all-night sub and gyro joint, her shopping spree apparently not quite done.

Working nights early in the week is mostly thankless drudgery— watching the needle on the fuel gauge creeping southward while counting and recounting the stack of singles that just won't multiply. There's always, mercifully, the one pickup that you decide is the last of the night. Mine's waving in front of a corner bar across the street. I hang a U-turn just as she crosses over to my side of the street. Completing the circle, she jumps in, shivering from the whipping wind. "Do you usually work these hours, are you a night owl?" she asks.

"Yup, vampire hours," I answer. Getting a laugh out of a pretty girl from this tired line makes the preceding hours almost worth it.

TUESDAY

The fish begin to bite a bit more on a Tuesday. There are still gaps between fares, but with a little inclement weather and some luck, a cabbie can walk away at the end of the shift with a few bucks in his pocket.

Banter

After the snow stops, the melting and graying begins. A woman stands on the curb, in the narrow break between two drifts, separated from the cab door by a dark moat of slush and grime. "Thirteen hundred North Astor at the corner of Gertuh, or Gothee," she says after finally braving that chasm, re-soaking her black boots, as evidenced by the jagged line of salt residue spanning heel to toe. That she felt the need to pronounce Goethe in both the German and the Chicago way is an instant conversation starter. She's a teacher at Roberto Clemente (pronounced Clement*ee*, not Clement*ay*), so correct pronunciation is a point of pride.

"No one knows where I live if I don't say it both ways." Neither of us is a native, so naturally the odd local ways of pronouncing Paulina and Devon (*Paul-eye-nuh* and *Duh-von*) are discussed, among others. Then to cap it off, there's an agreeable evisceration of Boston, Massachusetts, a town upon which the heaping of scorn is a

time-honored tradition in my taxi. Most who have had the misfor-
tune of living there feel the same and earn points by commiserating.
This is one of those rare conversations that break the barrier between
driver and passenger. Nothing earth-shaking or portending of anything further, just banter to be savored for its own simple qualities.

"Thank you for rescuing me from that ridiculous street, just
couldn't deal with those puddles anymore." She smiles and heads
into her high-rise, the path mercifully free and clear.

The girl is in a hurry to drop off her rent check into the mail slot of the realty office before continuing on elsewhere. "My boyfriend usually takes care of it, but I started getting calls about it and, guess what, he didn't. Gotta love THAT!" We swap deadbeat roommate stories, the former friends lost over piddling sums, such a common experience that we all store rants on the subject, to be rolled out for occasions such as this one.

"I have to ask friends of friends to remind them, like, dude, you owe me money!" she says, laughing, then jumps out to meet up with her prince.

Their address is on Sawyer, yet I sit on Spaulding, the same street number but half a block west. Looking at the two-flat, then at the information on the screen, including "Apt. #2W," it occurs to me that if there's only one place on the second floor, it wouldn't be designated west or east. Hauling ass to the right spot, they're just coming out as I pull up. We share a laugh over the mistake, apparently it happens all the time. On another day this might lead to tense minutes of silence for the duration of the trip, while today it's no matter at all.

None of this is of much consequence aside from the fact that the job so often exposes people in a less than flattering light, and sometimes a bit of small talk can be just what we need. So much of this job is like going on safari or to some far-flung planet, the manners and ways of the inhabitants a hopelessly indecipherable mystery. It's a relief to talk without worrying about dialect or proper diction, to be understood for a moment, no matter how slight the subject at hand might be.

Drug Run

A man calls for a taxi from an all-night diner on Archer. Shaking, sweating, and shifty-eyed, he directs me to the West Side. Over the Eisenhower, north on Pulaski, we slow for him to look over the merchants: guys that hide their faces in hoodies, shout out to passing cars, and signal their crew if there is a bite. "You know what's going on here, right?" he asks, and I tell him not to say it. He tosses me a twenty as down payment.

We pull into the parking lot of a fried fish joint, and he rolls down his window and conducts his business.

Now he's in a hurry to get out of there and return to that Archer diner. He keeps asking if I'm OK with where we've gone; when he pays me about double what's on the meter, it definitely makes it easier to take. He walks into the over-lit restaurant still sweating buckets, though that'll pass in minutes, now that he's scored.

Supernumerary

She bounds toward the cab from the Lyric Opera House. A thin middle-aged woman in a white turtleneck, pants, and a Bears cap. "I got the part!

"This was my fifth try, and I finally got it. I'm going to be onstage

in the opera! . . . No, I won't be singing. Know what a supernumerary is? It's like an extra. They need them for every production, and it's an exclusive club; once you're in, you're in!" Her eyes glow as she looks out the window, pondering her suddenly bright future.

"This was one of my life's goals. To be near the divas when they sing. When I turned fifty, I told myself, 'I'm going to learn to appreciate opera.' It took a few years, but I just love it now . . . Can't help thinking that this is a reward for surviving breast cancer . . . Boy! How am I gonna be able to teach tomorrow? Probably won't sleep tonight!"

She teaches computer science at Northwestern, and a pop quiz will have to do for the next day because she won't be capable of more under the circumstances. She talks of climbing Kilimanjaro, of riding her Harley all over the West, and of how this day ranks right up there with all of them.

"I'll have to wear a ring to discourage the men. Not doing it for dating, not ready for that with the cancer and all, you understand? . . . Already see Joe sniffing around, being extra friendly. Got a plain gold band, it'll do. Can't blame them for trying. They see a fifty-year-old woman jumping around like that, they think, 'WOW look at her! She's like a twenty-year-old!' "

I confess that I have no patience for opera, can never understand why they have to make those awful sounds come out of their throats. She insists that I haven't given it enough time. "It's a stylized, artificial art like ballet, and there's nothing more beautiful when done right." She's impressed that a family friend of mine has actually starred at the Lyric, even though I admit to barely making it to intermission when seeing her sing. Nothing I or anyone else might say could dampen my passenger's joy.

"Oh, I can't wait to see what Daryl the doorman will say! When you see the banner for the Lyric's next season, think of me!" She beams, then turns away toward the glass revolving doors of her high-rise, just off Lake Shore Drive.

The sun is setting and my goals are more modest than hers. The cabdriver's role is to play a bit part in others' lives and be compensated accordingly.

Fog

Fog comes in and hides the skyscrapers just as the last of the graying milky daylight fades. Streetlamps light no more than a few feet in any direction before being consumed by the murky cotton wadding that now binds all forms together. Streets driven thousands of times bear no resemblance to their former selves, transformed into stage sets for Gothic tales—or slasher flicks depending on one's age and taste. The change isn't entirely unwelcome. After all, it's not every day that the back of your hand changes into an inscrutable riddle.

The first passengers to take note of the weather are four Native Americans returning from the North Side to the Marriott on Michigan Avenue. In town from all over the country for that weekend's Powwow, they speak of life on the Res and ask the usual Chicago tourist questions—no use telling them that the Sears Tower has lost its name since their last visit and that the man who'd designed it had

passed away this very day. Instead I tell them how to get to Pizzeria Uno from their hotel and point out where the lake would usually appear out the left windows as we take Lake Shore Drive south. Not only is there no lake, but northbound traffic isn't much more than disembodied headlights, gone as soon as they appear. My passengers don't believe that the entrance we stop at leads to their lodgings; it takes some reassuring before they are convinced to disembark. It just isn't a night for certainty.

A girl heading to Lakeview questions the route I'm taking, remaining dubious despite a detailed and logical explanation. Being second-guessed doesn't do much for anyone's disposition, so a tense silence follows. "Look at all this fog," she says, voice filled with wonder as she looks out the window to where the lake once was. The bad feelings dissipate into awe. The car ahead of us feels with its front wheels for the proper lane, sensing it to either side, as a blind man does with his cane, slowing then speeding, trying in vain to maintain a steady clip. She asks how I like driving in this, and I answer that "like" and "drive" don't often sit in the same sentence no matter the condition of the road. We part as friends.

Landmarks leave no trace. Navy Pier is swallowed whole and the less-than-charitable thought that with luck it might not reappear once this pea soup lifts has to be abandoned when the famous Ferris wheel comes into view. No skyline, no grid, only the nearest corners of buildings, with no apparent tops or sides visible in the gaseous drifts; this Tuesday made strange by nature.

Crack

Double-parked by the darkened courtyard building in Garfield Park, I key in the Auto Callout code to summon my passenger. A group of young men loiter by the chain-link that surrounds the liquor store next door. They play-punch one another and otherwise horse around to break up the monotony and keep the chill out of their bones. The minutes lurch forward with no sign of my guy, and I put in the code for a "No Show."

Before I can pull away, a woman runs out from the farthest doorway and begs me to wait. "He's comin'; it just take him a while," she says, then disappears back into the murk. A man in a red-and-white track suit edges into view, moving along the wall of the building, stopping every few feet to gather himself before going on. Cracking the back door, he sucks the air in like a beached carp. He wheezes for me to stay put. " All right, I need you to take me to the hospital to get a new oxygen tank, then take me back, cool? First though, we got to find this guy, he's got somethin' of mine. Just go ahead, I'll tell you where."

We go west, slowing at alleys for no apparent reason, on a hunt with rules beyond my comprehension. Occasionally he barks out at passing men, their faces hidden in oversize hoodies—"Hey, where D? Know where he at?"—with no satisfactory answers forthcoming. After about twenty minutes, I tell him that I've got places to be, that rolling around with him all night's not an option. He seems to understand and agrees to just go to the hospital and grab another cab back. "Let's just check this one place first."

That "one place" is another slum a couple miles southwest of where we'd been straying. Pools of broken glass collect near the curbs and reflect the headlight beams as we turn from one broken-down block to the next. Past unmarked squad cars out for bigger game, past pedestrians likely out looking for some elusive prize, past loiterers leaning on vehicles stilled for good. Protesting again about time lapsing, I manage to get us steered back homeward. Just then, he sees some invisible sign in the sidewalk that commands him urgently down the next unlit street. "This is it, I swear!"

We pull up to a two-flat, and he rolls down the window, summoning a man from the rocking chair on the porch. After some whispered negotiations, the new guy gets in and gives the street corner they want. Cop cars and paddy wagons whiz by at breakneck speeds. "Somebody got they asses shot for sure" is the verdict from the backseat. We turn off California a block from where all the sirens have come to rest. Here, a group based on the stoop of a boarded-up brownstone is doing a brisk business, passing baggies in exchange for bills to all comers. The loudly marked taxi causes the young entrepreneurs a bit of pause, assuaged quickly by the crumpled fives passed through the rolled-down rear window, and then we're off.

After splitting their purchases, we drop his partner off and head back to his place. The trip to that hospital is no longer necessary; in fact, he wants to double back for another hit of the medicine doled from the stoop. He doesn't protest much when I refuse. We end up back at that courtyard, same fellas still hanging around, apparently unable to meet my customer's discriminating needs. On his way out, in appreciation, he offers, "You're the type'a guy, people can't help but like ya!" and with that he creeps away, hugging the bricks back to the entryway to his abode. That oxygen tank won't be needed now.

Veteran

Outside the Continental at 2:30 a.m., he pulls up behind me. "Anybody in there?"

Waiting for the late-night revelers on a Tuesday night can be a test of endurance. Luckily, my newly arrived compatriot is willing to part

with a smoke in exchange for a dollar, marking the occasion by also lighting up.

"Been driving cab since '73 and've never seen it this bad," he offers, his scraggly white beard yellowed around the mouth from nicotine. Thick glasses slipping down the bridge of his nose reveal watery eyes. Despite the mild temperature, his winter coat is buttressed by a vest, sweatshirt, and untold other hidden layers. "Had one radio call since 9 p.m., I owe 'em $20 for last night. Tomorrow I gotta go to the doctor, but I might blow it off because there may not be enough for the bus fare. I need to feed my animals too . . ."

He's been writing science-fiction stories on a manual typewriter for years, though with no luck getting anything published. The latest involves a human-size insect who's also a detective. This insect-detective discovers the remains of a person's arm, chiseled to the sharpest point ever detected on his planet. "The 'e' has given out, and I don't know if anybody can fix it. Used to have an old guy, whole house filled with typewriters; gone now. Wanted to sign up for computer classes at the Senior Center on Lawrence and Damen, but the waiting list is five months long."

He swings the door out, followed by a cane from the passenger's seat, and puts a foot on the ground. Just then, the Gandalf dispatch system emits a sustained beep, alerting him that a fare is waiting; he reverses the steps with deliberation and a lack of breath, then pulls away, saying, "Norwegian Hospital" by way of a good-bye. Two satiated patrons finally emerge from the Continental, and I drive them to a downtown hotel. An hour and half's worth of purgatory is quickly converted into $12.50.

WEDNESDAY

This day can go either way: you can rake it in or struggle just to make your expenses. A wild card of a day that can push the rest of the week into the red or the black depending on how it breaks.

Breakdown

I get to the garage at 6:30 a.m., hoping to beat the rush. All my cab needs is for the AC to get fixed—it is just blowing hot air. How long should a job like that take? An hour or two, right? Wrong.

They start right away, and I spend the first couple of hours painting a picture of cabs inside the garage. By the third hour, I periodically wander over to look toward my cab, which is being attended to by a kid who looks to be about twelve. Sometimes it's raised on the lift, other times back down. Other mechanics come by to consult or offer encouragement. When questioning the shop manager, no definitive answers can be gleaned.

In case of breakdowns, the driver is instructed to inform the cashier and to give them the cab's meter, thereby putting him in line to get the next available cab or to be compensated for lost time. Of course I didn't do this, figuring it would be a quick job, so when

asking the manager if there might still be a few pennies thrown my way, his answer isn't much of a surprise. Cab companies make sure the driver gets the short end of the stick; it's practically in our lease agreement.

At the fourth hour, the mechanics break for lunch, my cab remaining in the same spot with the hood up. By then, I'd positioned myself with a clear line of vision trained on my teenage tormentor and his seemingly futile efforts. At hour seven, the manager takes mercy and after a stern talking-to about proper procedures, issues a shop credit. Shortly after that I'm back behind the wheel.

Fifteen minutes after turning on the AC, the car is overheating and there's a new squeaking sound coming from the vicinity of the front right wheel. Without the AC on, it runs OK, about the same as before it was ever brought in.

The Voice of America

I pick him up at the bar on the corner of Damen and 18th, the one with the model trains in the window. "What's the dollar extra for?" he asks after lumbering into the backseat.

"Gas surcharge," I say, spurring a look of disbelief and a response implying: *$3.25 just to sit my ass down!?!*

"There ain't no gas shortage, just a lot of greed, and these politicians are in on it . . . If McCain wins, nothing will change, and the other one's a monkey, in more ways than one . . . It's not the same America anymore, more like the United States of Zimbabwe . . . I used to drive in New York, and I'd get into fights with 'em just for fun, the Africans and the Arabians."

We stop briefly at a service station, where he gets out and peels off some bills for a mechanic in the garage, then huffs and puffs before settling back into the passenger seat.

"Know any good Indian restaurants near Union Station?" he asks, then consults the White Pages he has with him, settles on an address, and directs me onward. "Most places by me are all grease. If it was up to me, they'd blow up all the McDonald's, so when

I'm downtown I figure I'll try something different. I own a coupla tow trucks—let others do the driving—but maybe I'll get my license back one of these days . . . Trying to start up an Internet thing too, drop-shipping—electronics and baby supplies, they're pretty hot these days."

We pull up to his Indian restaurant, which turns out to be a Jewish deli. Doing his best Pakistani accent, he conveys his appreciation for having an American cabdriver for a change, slowly gathers his belongings and proceeds out to have his "ethnic" meal.

You Know Where I'm Going

I pick him up at the Gas For Less station on Lincoln. He is overweight and a little disheveled but otherwise doesn't seem unusual.

He gets in and says, "You know where I'm going." I don't and tell him so. What follows is a back-and-forth lasting a good five minutes;

he can't believe it; he is convinced I know . . . Meanwhile the meter is running as we drive west on Irving Park for want of a more precise destination. Finally, he makes peace with my ignorance and launches into a rambling account of his life story; our friendship sealed by the $20 he gives me. He tells me about how his family has been in Chicago a long time, pointing out buildings they've owned along the way. We're heading south on Pulaski now. He says that he's had some problems, has been living in Indianapolis, but is back in town to perform his one-man show impersonating Chris Farley at Second City. Periodically through this saga he would ask how much money he'd given me, growing more satisfied each time I repeated the same answer; we're now best buddies. By and by, he breaks down and tells me where he wants to go.

We pull up in front of the Lathrop Homes projects at Diversey and Damen. It's after 5 p.m., rush hour, and the guys hanging out front are doing a brisk business. My friend hands me another $20 and tells me to wait, running out in the direction of the young men. After a bit of back-and-forth, he's pointed toward a window at which he proceeds to scream at the top of his lungs, "GIVE ME DRUGS!!!!!"

The two guys look over at me with a look that says, *What have you unleashed on us?* It's about then that I decide there had been enough entertainment for the evening and tear out of there without looking back.

Wrong Moves

A middle-aged suit-and-tied black gentleman gives directions from Ukrainian Village to River North. Two blocks from his destination, we detour to the CITGO for cigarettes, where he chats up a young woman who is loitering outside. From the cadence of her voice, it's clear that she's either a junkie or a mental defective, but most likely a bit of both. They return to the cab as intimates, their hushed talk continuing en route. They get out near a motel, his eyes not meeting mine as he gives an overgenerous tip.

They recap their evening spent playing Rock Band in giddy tones. Two guys in their twenties, drunk but not hammered, clearly loving

life. "Shit. She asked me to pick up double-stick tape, but they only had Krazy Glue—you think it'll be OK?" one of them wonders aloud; apparently his fiancée asked him to run the errand, and it had slipped his mind. They debate whether she'd care or not, seeing as their wedding is tomorrow; is it a deal-breaker? "Don't worry about it, dude," his friend concludes. "She loves you, and there's practically no difference between the two."

A young man in aviator shades flags me down at 23rd and Western. His buddy was locked up for a DUI, and he was there to bail him

out. The charges were upgraded because the genius had floored it right in front of a police station, so there would be no walking out today. In his despair, he's decided to get wasted at a Mexican joint, leaving $50 on a $20 tab. As we ride down Western, he tells me to stop at a liquor store, his pal's plight overwhelming him. He invites me to go to the movies, saying a bucket of buttered popcorn would go great with Ketel One Vodka, but though I'm a fan of both, I have to politely decline. His girlfriend calls then, asking him to come over and bring some condoms, so I'm off the hook.

They shove her in the backseat against her wishes. She'd been in the middle of the street outside the Continental, yelling at passing cars and dancing drunkenly. They've had it and ask that she be taken home. It is somewhere less than a mile away, which is as specific as it ever gets because all my questions are met with silence or incoherent babbling; the word *address* is answered with phrases like "I am address, NO . . . why are you mad at me? I don't want it." Asking for her wallet for clues, she produces her makeup case instead. There's

no choice but to go back to the bar where her friends welcome her with less-than-open arms.

Customer of the Month

Mounds of plowed packed snow narrow the street to one car's width, so when the headlights near in the rearview mirror, it's necessary to pull up to the cross street to let them pass. A little guy appears as I'm reversing the cab back to the address, follows alongside, and gets in as it comes to rest. "Twenty-first and Michigan," he says, then returns to a very much out-loud inner monologue.

Moans and retching sounds punctuate his oratory; the feeble radio talk show volume can hardly compete. Mental images of vomit on the backseat cannot be kept at bay. The cleanup and confrontation to follow feels like a dread certainty. "The Jewel on Roosevelt and Clark," he commands, interrupting the demons midsentence.

It is really at the corner of Wabash, so after making it clear that was what he wanted, we pull into the grocery store's lot. "I'll be right out," he yells, getting out on the driver's side into oncoming traffic and bolting through the automatic sliding doors.

An examination of the rear seat turns up no mess, only a scattering of his belongings. An asthma inhaler placed into the handle of the door, crumpled singles (immediately confiscated with foresight), a stocking cap, two clear baggies containing little white pills, a shopping bag with a key ring and used napkins, and an occasionally vibrating cell phone.

Twenty minutes crawl by, the meter ticking away as late-night shoppers run in and out of the store, and no sign of the guy. Finally he appears, at the tail end of the only open checkout line. Moments later he's being half-dragged/half-carried by the scruff of the neck, in the paws of the hulking security guard, who's trailed by a displeased cashier.

Gathering his crap, I head inside, knocking on the unmarked door into which they'd disappeared. His screamed protests supply the soundtrack, as I hand his belongings over to the cashier. "He don't have no money for no cab," she kindly offers, before wishing me a good night.

Deluge

I pull up to the 7-Eleven, driving a guy on a mission to get Ben & Jerry's. Lightning lights up the night as rain alternates with hail, pelting the cab and making visibility barely a hope. The couple stands cowering in the doorway, obviously stranded by the deluge. I roll the

window down enough to tell them I'll be back, as my fare is only going a couple blocks farther.

I maneuver around downed light poles and trees, through newly formed lakes, and back to that store; they huddle together as before. His stop is first, and they kiss for a minute or two before he runs to his door. She apologizes for the necking as we pull away, to which I reply that as long as the backseat is left as they'd found it, there is no problem. First date? Of course it was. They'd remember it too, as the day the sky fell to earth.

She'd known him for three years and suspected that they'd both harbored a secret crush for that long. She'd been reading a Russian novel called *Three Seconds' Silence* about a sailor in a storm. This inspired her that day to bite the bullet and ask him out. Without turning back to look, it is obvious that she's glowing; it had gone so much better than she imagined. "We were wondering if we'd even make it home, could've stayed in front of the 7-Eleven making out all night."

She pays and runs across Halsted to her place. I go on. Through blacked-out city blocks, windshield wipers failing to keep up, squeals issuing from the soaked undercarriage of the cab, the night a bit brighter despite all evidence to the contrary.

THURSDAY

This is the start of the weekend for some. The bars won't be as full as on Friday or Saturday, but there's often steady work from the afternoon on. Some begin their celebrations early; others wait until the wee hours. Thursday is the day the search for companionship (or just a warm body) begins in earnest.

Ohio House

The man asks to be taken to the Westin Hotel off Michigan Avenue. He talks about living here years ago in that nostalgic way that hints at wild times and freedom long since traded for comfort. As we wait for the green at Ohio and LaSalle, he looks out the window at the northwest corner and says, "My uncle used to own that place in the '70s before selling it to the Archdiocese of Chicago." He's pointing at the triple stack of diamonds comprising the sign of the Ohio House Motel.

"That coffee shop's one of those greasy spoons that you leave actually covered in grease," he jokes, before abandoning the subject.

I drop him off, but his story lingers. Who knew whether it was truth or tall tale? A '50s-era motor lodge overshadowed by the supersize McDonald's to the east and other chain eateries assaulting the eyes in every direction, the Ohio House would be a better fit on some secondary roadway far outside of town. Yet there it is on the Ohio feeder off the Kennedy Expressway, waiting for vehicles slowing to surface-street speed. To the tourists trapped in the

bottleneck, it whispers of seedy doings from long ago, its perpetually half-filled parking lot suggesting that business is somewhat less than booming.

Before the old owner's nephew, my last fare to remark on the place had been four frat boys gloating about the stripper they'd stashed in a room there as part of a bachelor party weekend. The timid ritual transgressions of their last hurrah seemed third- or fourth-rate, older even than the roadside landmark that hosted them.

Those flattened diamond shapes, echoed multiple times along the roof and elsewhere in the design, burn onto the retina and repeat, fading into the back of my brain without ever truly disappearing.

Love Hotel

I pick them up in Wrigleyville after another Cubs loss. An average-looking couple, probably in their early thirties; they want to go to Union Station, so off we go. No more than a minute in, the girl's head disappears from view, followed by some rustling around, movement, and adjustments. Three-quarters of the way there, the girl pops up and asks if they can go to Downers Grove instead of the train station. After that, the guy surfaces to ask whether it's OK if they "play around," to which I wonder aloud why he'd ask now, seeing that they were pretty far along already. As long as they leave the place the way they found it, I'm fine with it. Hearing what he wanted to hear, he goes back under.

As we get on the highway, a flip-flop-clad foot appears in my rearview mirror. It moves along the ceiling trying to find the right spot, eventually settling on the rear window of the cab. Thereafter, various body parts flicker in and out of view. I try to concentrate on the White Sox game on the radio.

As we near downtown Downers Grove, the happy couple re-appears in a more or less standard passenger's pose; seated upright, that is. We get stuck at the rail crossing, where I have the chance to ask whether the Metra conductors would allow them to do on the train what they'd just finished doing in my cab. They both laugh and say they're just happy to have some alone time away from the children. The husband seems especially pleased with himself, re-peating over and over how now that they've *just finished fucking in a cab*, it's time to walk around with the kids. They thank me profusely and leave a $30 tip.

The Sox won too.

The Check

He floats down the steps of a downtown high-rise and gives direc-tions to a bank about a mile away. Halfway there he says, "Shit!!! Can we go back?" After retrieving what he'd left behind, we head back to the bank again and he tells me his story.

Five years ago, he'd been at a nightclub downtown when a fight erupted. His retina was severed by a flying piece of glass. Multiple surgeries and court appearances had finally led him to this moment in this cab. The high-rise was where his lawyer's office is, and the item we'd had to return for was his settlement check.

He shows it to me, beaming. All the aggravation has finally paid off: $469,000. He says he's planning to put most of it away, though we're headed to the bank to cash it. The only thing I can tell him is to beware of new friends and long-lost relatives coming out of the woodwork. He couldn't have been more than twenty-five. I'd never seen that many zeros on a check other than in the movies.

He leaves a good tip as I wish him well, then he floats toward the bank's doors.

Nose Job

She stands outside Helen's Two Way Lounge, squinting through tinted glasses in the afternoon sun to make sure the cab is really for her.

"Go down Fullerton, *not* Armitage. I got this route all worked out . . .
Running late, but he knows me, I'm always late, he'll understand."
Four in the afternoon and her words slurred as if it were four in the
morning. Her name is Trish, and she wants to know all about me.

Finding out I'm Jewish, she exclaims, "Me too! Well, I'm Catho-
lic and Jewish. I think the Catholics and Jews are a lot alike; it's the
Christians like Baptists that I don't understand . . . I mean if Hitler
was here right now, you know where I'd be going, right? Look at this

nose. If you knew anything about geology, you'd know I was Jewish!" She ponders these matters quietly for a few moments before adding, "I had an opportunity to get a nose job for free once, but my girlfriend got one and they fucked it all up." She makes me turn around so she can demonstrate how the lip had somehow been sewn to the nostril. "I'm better off with what God gave me, right?"

She wishes me a good day and creeps across Armitage to Shoe's, one of the few odd old man bars left in Lincoln Park, to continue her lost afternoon.

Whisperer

An older woman waits on the edge of the parking lot of a community center on Chicago Avenue amid shimmering pools of broken

glass. With her white hair tied back in a grandmotherly bun, she doesn't look like she belongs on this woebegone stretch of the West Side until she begins to speak— or whisper, more accurately.

I have to turn off the radio, roll up the windows, and practically hold my breath to make out what few directions she offers. Going south on Pulaski, she wants me to turn right on Kinzie, but "slowly, slowly . . ." We pass various salvage emporiums; this is where the trucks trawling the city's alleys must haul some of their treasures to be converted to cash. Freight tracks ran along the right side of the road, and a ragged man, perched on the concrete divider, is taking a hammer to some object that only he can discern.

The 10 mph pace does not inspire her to any more precise instructions. We turn into the Northwest Industrial Park, passing warehouses, city fleet facilities, and multiple tractor-trailers backing laboriously into bays to unload their cargo. Finally reaching a cul-de-sac turnaround, she says to stop. She pays up and wanders away distractedly, only to return when she notices me idling while making a phone call. "You have to move along—you're blocking traffic here," she hisses, jerking her arms as if to clear room on the roadway. After watching to make sure I'd pulled away down the carless street, she turns back and tentatively steps toward the garbage-strewn lot that is the endpoint of her trek.

Senior Citizen

The wind nearly blows the old woman off her feet as the doorman and the caretaker struggle to put her in the back of the taxi. She fights against their help, telling them she can do it herself, spending what

little energy she has waving her arms for freedom. The Filipino aide comes around and gets in on the other side and is promptly informed, "I don't want you along. I want to go by myself. Symphony Hall, driver. You know where that is? It's across from the Art Institute."

The four or five blocks from the East Randolph Street high-rise to the Michigan Avenue drop-off are spent with the two women bickering. The fare is $4.15, and the old woman makes a show of digging through her purse, eventually pulling out a bank deposit envelope. The three singles it contains seem to puzzle her; she shuffles them several times as if hoping to make more appear. She asks her companion if she has any cash. "You know I never carry cash" is the aide's angry answer. I tell her to just give me what she has and to move along, at which the aide spits out, "She *has* money—she just don't want to pay!" while the old lady does her best impression of dementia-induced confusion.

Extricating her from the backseat takes several more minutes. She wants my number so I can come pick her up at the end of the performance, which I flatly refuse; getting played by her twice in one day would exceed my reserve of goodwill. She makes a show of acting hurt, then leans on her cane and starts toward the symphony's doors. "Bless you," the Filipina calls out as I pull away.

Street Meat

He flags me down in Old Town, a pipsqueak of a man wearing thick glasses. We head west on North Avenue, and he asks whether the hookers still hang out here. "I used to get blown for twenty dollars by the underpass . . . Me and my buddies used to call 'em *Street Meat*," he says proudly, as if he'd coined the term. "They've really cleaned it up around here," he adds, with regret in his voice. When I tell him that most Yuppies preferred to be serviced at home these days, he protests that he likes to get his off the side of the road. He pays and runs across the street to an upscale nightspot.

A tiny Asian girl gets in at 3 a.m. in Ukrainian Village, going downtown. She lists the services that she will and will not perform to someone on the receiving end of her cell. "I'm a nursing student. No, I'm

on my way to a date now. Wanna meet later? What do you look like?"
She gets out at a big apartment building with a doorman, near the lake.

Girls of all sizes and shapes call to be taken to work at VIP's or the Admiral, the last two big strip clubs in the city. They're usually silent during the ride, perhaps steeling themselves for the night ahead; it's hard to be friendly off-duty when you have to fake it for hours on end to make a living. The Admiral offers free admission to cabdrivers, as well as a $10 bonus for steering customers their way. The two professions seem linked somehow, especially in the eyes of out-of-towners—they think that we have stables of willing ladies just waiting to help them cheat on their wives.

On the West Side in the middle of a snowstorm, the girl is so grateful to finally get a cab. She is a young heavily made-up Latina on her way to the Belden-Stratford, a posh old residential hotel in Lincoln Park. There is no pretense here—she tells me how badly she needs this trick. The guy is a repeat customer. She sympathizes with me, having to be out in this mess. We pull into the drive, and shortly after, an obese older gentleman in a robe comes out, pays the fare, and escorts her inside.

With their makeup, voices, and flamboyant clothes, none of the four could definitively be classified as either female or male; they are in that sweet spot calculated to appeal to the widest potential clientele.

They run over from their perch in the Punkin' Donuts parking lot at Belmont and Clark, where they'd been all night, talking up the lonely people trolling for love. They sing along to B96 as we hit Lake Shore Drive and keep it up all the way down to the Dan Ryan. We exit on 63rd Street, and they're all suddenly silent except for occasional instructions to turn left or right. Then we stop at an abandoned lot, the cab doors fly open, and they scatter in all directions.

Good-bye, Nerd

On a Thursday night outside Buddy Guy's Legends, a man crouches slightly with his left hand extended uncertainly, possibly needing a ride. He pushes past the couple at the curb and into the backseat and barks, "Get on the Eisenhower. Going to Oak Park."

His eyes wander away from each other toward opposite ends of his face, spittle glistens from his patchy beard, his hair greased back, teeth crooked and gapped. "They oughta know how to fight, wasn't doin' nothin', fuckin' nerds. What a joke ha-ha-ha-ha . . . knew a guy once who married a nerd, never amount to nothing."

What follows his statement is a series of alternately guttural and whining animal noises apparently continuing a conversation with someone only he can see.

Off the Austin exit, his last-second instruction is to turn left; he barely bothers because staring out the window and intoning, "Goodbye, nerd; good-bye, nerd; good-bye, nerd," at all passersby is of far higher priority. Locking eyes briefly in the rearview mirror, he suddenly asks matter-of-factly about how the night's going. This is more unnerving in its way than the incoherent babble that came before.

We roll westbound on Roosevelt through Berwyn, then left on Harlem, passing the town Welcome sign for Riverside. Two municipalities past his stated destination, I ask whether we're close and he answers, "I'll show you."

Approaching the train tracks, he suddenly wants me to pull over; this I accomplish by rudely cutting off an eighteen-wheeler. That's how ready I am to be rid of him. Fully ready to be stiffed or worse, the long minutes of fumbling through his pockets yield a crumpled $20 along with six ones. "It's all I got," he says, to which I offer no argument, more than grateful not to end up a severed head in his icebox. He crosses through braking traffic toward the light of a tavern.

FRIDAY

Friday afternoons they flee their offices, anxious to do whatever they can't while at work. Getting them *from* and *to* can add up to a living for many a driver. Of course, this is also when the serious overindulging begins, so those dollars can sometimes feel more like combat pay. For those of us interested in observing the mating rituals and other characteristic behaviors of the urban male and female, there's no better seat in the house.

Flood

The sun attacks the cab's windshield from a nearly cloudless sky on Friday afternoon, roasting the interior and making the AC strain to its limit, as the two women pile in towels, coolers, four children, and folding chairs en route to North Avenue Beach. They laugh and talk all the way, paying no heed to the gradual darkening up above. By the time we pull up to the mouth of the beach's parking lot, the first drops wet the windows.

Three young guys climb in before the ladies have even removed the last of their belongings, asking to go to Lakeview. Nearing the Belmont exit off Lake Shore Drive, the rain picks up, robbing most motorists of the rudimentary driving skills adequate to fairer conditions. The pace slows to a crawl, and drivers' awareness of details such as lanes and reasonable following distances fall away in favor of white-knuckled survival techniques. My passengers are oblivious to all of this, preoccupied as they are with an in-depth analysis of the underage girls they'd been chatting up by the lakefront volleyball courts. Side streets eventually get us to their destination just as winds begin to whip the downpour sideways and the sky turns a sick green-gray.

The Cubs game has just ended, which would have made the neighborhood hectic regardless, but combined with the deluge, all unable to find shelter lunge toward any passing taxi like castaways reaching for the last remaining life raft. The two who get to me next are well-lubricated and cracking each other up as we creep westward. The wipers are mostly useless as the force of the torrent allows only the barest outlines of parked cars to remain visible. The taillights ahead serve as the only evidence of roadway. The two-mile trip takes about half an hour. I drive up onto the curb so they won't drown in the lake that has formed by the door to their condo, earning a few extra dollars' appreciation.

Underpasses fill like moats, slowing passage further. Trees splinter, unable to withstand the gales, smashing car hoods and blocking one-way streets. By the time the storm lets up, it feels like it has been beating down on the city for hours when it has only been about forty minutes. The sun reemerges and weary people creep out, shaking off the water like half-drowned rats. The gridlock continues for some time, making good service impossible and causing restiveness in the clientele—several times I have to tell a girl banging her foot against the partition to stop or walk the rest of the way, while a fellow decides that since we're momentarily idled at a stoplight, he must be home and proceeds to swing the door open just as we start to move again. Perhaps like a full moon the atmospheric conditions fool with their inner equilibrium, but whatever the reason, it makes for a tiring evening of driving. By ten or eleven when the heavens open up once more, it's like bracing for one last counterpunch in a twelve-round bout.

Those lucky enough to dodge the raindrops upon leaving the bars and Friday soirées remain largely unaware of the damage. Some wonder why their apartments stand dark as they get out of the cab, joining some half a million residents experiencing power outages. Friday nights are for washing away the weight of the week, and no flooding, however biblical in scope, will thwart the determined weekend warrior from slogging through another eve of inebriation. The job is to ferry them from one oasis to the next whether the route is smooth or pitted and obstructed as it was on this night. Coming through it unscathed would count as some consolation were it not for the fact that the trick would need to be repeated the next night and the night after that with or without the cooperation of Mother Nature.

He Hit Me

She sits on the front steps of a condo building. Her mouth is gaping open, but from a distance it isn't clear whether it's with joy or grief. When I stop and look closer, that mystery's soon solved.

She has coat hangers draped with a couple weeks' worth of outfits and a little dog milling about. The lights are on in the first-floor apartment, likely the place she's leaving. She's on her phone, and

with the window down I can hear her sobs. Gathering up her belongings, she makes her way to the cab.

Choked cries escape her for a couple minutes before a destination
can be determined. "He hit me," she says. "He's never done that
before . . ." They'd been going out only a few months, but this night
he was drunk and he hit her in the face. There's no visible bruise, but
she's in shock.

Earlier that night I'd resolved not to buy any more cigarettes, but
when she asks for one, I pull over at the closest gas station and we
both light up. It seems to calm her a bit, though she's still shaking
slightly. I try to convince her that we aren't all like him. She doesn't
reply.

She gets out at a loft-style condo building in the old meatpacking district, fumbling with her keys for what seems like an eternity. Her presence stays in the taxi like a ghost for the rest of the night.

South Side

By the Pony Inn on Belmont he holds the door open, blocking traffic, sucking in the last few drags off a butt before getting in. "Don't sweat it, man, there's a big tip in it for you.

"Oh good, you're no A-rab! Got a deal for you: $50 to 111th and Western?" I agree to his terms, so he settles in to hold forth. "The

North Side's OK; lotsa stupid drunk bitches in all the bars. Look, I'm no player, but there were three hot chicks tryin' to make out with me. Where you live?" The answer makes him light up. "You ever come to the South Side? The hidden gem of the city—best people, all the cops, the firefighters, they all live around there—you're a Sox fan? Aww, man, you gotta come out some time!"

We're on the Ryan speeding south when he realizes his phone is dead and asks to use mine. "Tryin' to call my girl. See if she answers. What time is it? Out with her friends, probably wasted, they hate me cuz I haven't always been the best . . . See, I fucked around with a North Side girl for a while. *Way* hotter than my girl, but the personality of a piece of Styrofoam. When it comes down to it, ya gotta stick with a South Side girl. It's goin' pretty well now."

The off-ramps fly by before his sudden request for an exit swerves us off the highway. We head west toward Beverly, his beloved neighborhood, through an area that makes him cast his eyes about with no small amount of unease. "Damn shines dicin' on the corner and right near my 'hood, a damn shame.

"Your choice: cash or card? If it's cash, we gotta stop somewhere. Already spent $150 tonight, and I still gotta meet up with my girl and her cunt-bag friends. She'll be happy to see me; they won't . . . Oh well." He runs out to the 7-Eleven for the ATM. Back out, he looks around, then edges toward the shrubs at the corner of the store's lot to take a leak before thinking better of it. A flap is torn from the ass of his jeans, revealing blue-and-white horizontal striped boxers. "Sometimes you get the stupidest ideas before coming to your senses. This store's patrolled all the time. What do I do when Uncle Stupid busts me . . . My whole family's cops, they say, 'No way you're gonna be a cop,' so I go to law school. Lot more schoolin', I make the same paycheck. State's attorney, I got one rule: you got two strikes, you're going to jail. Makes sense, right?"

After a few final minute yet none-too-precise directions, we come to rest at the corner of 105th and Western. "Take $60, man, you earned it the way you hauled ass on that highway. I've taken this ride before, and with those towelheads it's all, yabba-dabba and shit, you're the best. Good convo, I mean it, man, you gotta come to the South Side."

Coming up to Damen Avenue Friday night after 1 a.m., driving west on Webster past the expressway underpass on the northern edge of Bucktown. Two squat forms wave, then shuffle up to the taxi. Both men look to be in their late forties: stout, compact, and bespectacled. The one without the thick black mustache asks for a Clark Street address in the Loop, so we hit the highway ramp and are off. The litany begins even before we merge into the downtown-bound traffic: "They don't like you, Bob; in fact, they hate your guts."

He has a speech impediment that turns his *r*'s and *l*'s into *w*'s, making him sound a bit like Elmer Fudd.

"They can't stand you. Admit it, they don't even like you," he continues, while Bob suffers in weary silence. "It's because you're a troublemaker, Bob. Why you have to be like that?"

Several variations on the theme follow, punctuated by emphatic gestures of pudgy hands, before Bob can stand it no more, asking in a gruff but quiet voice, "Why? Why don't they like me and they like you? I didn't do nothing to them."

His tormentor, snot running unrestrained from nose into mouth,

has a ready answer. "They see you bossing me around, they don't like it. Why you always boss me around, Bob? They like me because I buy 'em drinks. They don't like you at all. They can't stand you, Bob. Admit it."

There's a practiced, almost ritualized rhythm to the list of grievances. The plaintive tone is more child's whine than adult's vent; they've done this many times before, and both know their roles.

We pull up to a MEN ONLY sign on South Clark, starkly backlit in white, advertising a transients' hotel. It stands across the street from the Federal Corrections facility—an ominously sharp-angled concrete high-rise with vertical slits for windows. A rummy runs screaming incoherently toward the staircase below that sign, as Bob's companion pops out of the cab and goes inside. The Board of Trade is around the corner, and in the daytime the seedy, forlorn feel of this block is disguised by the bustle of the throngs. At 1:30 a.m. there's no such facade, the liquor store a few doors down providing the only oasis of activity.

Bob sits quietly waiting for his partner, who returns, panting. "He said they're at Midway." So it was back onto the freeway en route to the little airport on the Southwest Side.

The listing of Bob's faults resumes, and his only defense is to insert "I take care of you" occasionally amid his partner's assertions. At the curb on the desolate arrivals level at Midway, Bob gets on his phone, reciting landmarks such as the airline names listed above the locked sliding doors to someone on the other end. "Is this a bus terminal?" he asks me. Their friends are apparently at the bus stop, so we circle back down to the lower level, Bob narrating the trek with vivid descriptions of all that passes before his eyes out the left rear window. Two scruffy types approach and make as if to get into the taxi. "Can you take us to Toyota Park?" one asks.

I beg off. Bob pays up, asking for a receipt and inspecting it carefully, then wanders away with his friends in search of further transport. Why are they going to a soccer stadium in the suburbs before the break of dawn? Is Bob really such a bad guy? These as well as many other queries go unanswered. A cab ride allows but an obstructed glimpse into the lives of those conveyed, and to ask more would be to ask too much . . .

Shit Happens When You Party Naked

Outside the Continental at 3 a.m., her three friends pile in the back, while she sits up front. "How old do you think I am?" she asks, and when I say fourteen, she pushes for an honest answer. When my guess is twenty-three, she's offended. "*Omigod*, you think I'm that old?"

She's just dumped her boyfriend and feels guilty. Why? Because he'd broken up with her, but after they got back together, she left him just out of spite. She makes me turn my head and look at her friend in the back. "Isn't she beautiful?" she asks.

"Yes, she's beautiful," I answer.

Leaving him wasn't enough, though; she also slept with his best friend. "Shit happens when you party naked!" she tells me as they jump out of the cab on their way to Walgreen's to buy frozen pizza.

Riptide

Four a.m. outside Marie's Riptide Lounge. Coming off the Kennedy, the familiar waving figures attract my cab like a magnet.

Two girls and one guy. The first gets in, urging her friend to follow. The guy hops in, but the other girl keeps walking away.

The street's deserted, and though they're strangers, they decide to split the cab. He's a cop in the 'burbs; she works in a hospital on the South Side. He knows the place, a friend's mom works there.

"Small world, huh?" she says.

Her stop's first, but as we pull up the banter ceases, broken by the sucking and smacking sounds of a first kiss. She asks him up moments later.

It stays with me for weeks. A few drinks, a couple distant shared acquaintances, then an invitation to spend the night.

Is it really that simple?

Drive-Thru

After the bars close, it's time to eat. There are 24-hour greasy spoons, convenience stores with frozen pizzas and junk food, and places that

deliver late into the night, but most people can't wait that long, so it's off to the drive-thru.

McDonald's realized a while ago that the people staggering out of taverns were underserved (in their culinary options) and began to leave their drive-thrus open all night. They weren't the first— White Castle's been open round the clock forever, but they tend to be in poor or out-of-the-way neighborhoods while McDonald's are everywhere.

Typically, it'll come to my passengers as a brilliant brainstorm: *Let's go to the drive-thru!* They ask tentatively, fearing the worst. Then when I agree, they offer to buy me food, so grateful that their wishes are about to be fulfilled.

A girl who barely escaped the unwanted advances of some creep at a party, barely sober enough to get into the cab on her own, asks to go to McDonald's and promptly throws up most of her strawberry shake all over the backseat after taking just a few sips.

A middle-aged run-down woman with teeth missing offers to blow me in exchange for a ride. She stands just past the second window of the drive-thru where they hand out the food, hoping to capitalize on the generosity or desperation of the inebriated.

A homeless-looking man walks up and down the advancing line of cars asking for cheeseburgers. At the window the cashier implores

me not to have mercy on him as he's had six or seven burgers already. "He's not really hungry at all," she insists.

Walk-ups are forbidden, so many pay for a cab solely to go through the drive-thru. Apparently reaching through a car window is thought to keep the employees safe.

An angry man with a backpack marches right up to the window and demands service. The line of waiting cars and dumbfounded employees are of no concern to him. He wants his cheeseburger and that's all there is to it. Advancing gently forward, I nudge him out of the way. I want my cheeseburger more.

Two guys outside a White Castle nearly get themselves run over making my cab stop. They're loaded down with a king's ransom of fast food, which they tear into before their asses hit the backseat. I'd saved their lives, to hear them tell it. We head north on Western, and in between gnawing on sliders, one of them becomes suspicious. "You're going the wrong way, man." His friend tries to shut him up, but his doubts persist until we reach his front door. The lethal combination of booze and late-night grazing reverse north and south once more.

The nights often end picking French fries, pieces of processed cheese, and assorted sticky items out of the backseat. The remnants of another evening of revelry, these bits of food would hardly reveal the doings of those who had eaten them. In that spent inebriated state, we devolve into primitive foraging animals, drawn to those inviting neon lights and the parade of others lining up for the sustenance doled out through a sliding window.

SATURDAY

If a cabdriver can't make it on a Saturday, it's time to try some other line of work. It's also when the clientele will be drunker, stupider, and more belligerent than any other day except holidays. If one is inclined to despair of the species, this is the day to give up the ghost.

However, we've all got to get by, so it's time to get to it; we can take the rest of the week to restore our faith in humanity.

Uglyville

Every weekend trolleys roll around the city filled with revelers, stopping to spit them out at taverns, then gathering them back up, plying them with more drinks en route to the next watering hole. Passing them, as they creep along snail-like on their rounds, the mirth on board seems forced if not outright false. Whatever it is that these people do the rest of the week that inspires them to climb aboard makes me think it must be something fairly awful.

A girl in a salmon-hued form-fitting dress bends over in the bushes while others stagger about the still trolley. It's come to rest at a stop sign with no regard for those who may wish to use this quiet lane for passage. As I make a wide turn around it, narrowly avoiding oncoming traffic, two ladies hurl themselves into view, commanding my attention by frantically waving their arms, while

balancing on teetering heels. A brunette in black and a blonde in white, they should've had their own theme song. "Halsted and Armitage, please," the brunette says, then asks her fair-haired friend, "Are you gonna be OK? I totally saw that. What's his problem?" She stops her questions to take a call, after which her tone changes a bit. "I don't wanna be that kind of a friend, but he bought me dinner so I, like, owe it to him to meet up. He's at the Tonic Room. I don't even know where that is. I'll be home soon." With that, we watch the blonde stumble to her doorway and disappear inside.

"She's my best friend. We were on that booze bus down the street from where you got us. Someone threw a beer at her head, and her boyfriend laughed instead of standing up for her. Jesus, what are we, eighteen or something? A real Trolley to Uglyville. Some Shirley Temple–looking bitch accused me of making eyes at her husband. Is it my fault he was flirting with me?"

The blonde had dated the guy only four months but was already telling him that she loved him. He repaid her affection by staying out all night doing coke, making him an hour late for the brunch she'd arranged for her parents to meet him. She couldn't fathom why he'd light up a joint on the corner with his buddies in broad daylight. That afternoon they'd all started drinking early. "He isn't like that; it's just when he's around his douche-bag buddies, it brings out the worst in him," she insists. How they ended up on the trolley isn't ever made completely clear, but by the time the cup had hit her friend's head, they were all far past wasted. It wasn't that it hurt; it was his reaction that wounded—why would he revel in her misery?

Nothing is answered as we stop at the Tonic Room. "She should dump him, right?" The only answer is to nod and take her money. Her role in this whole thing, aside from that of unreliable narrator, is never revealed.

Too Much Information

Sometimes a guy will launch into his story with no prompting at all.

"What a weekend! My buddy, he's a federal judge, sets me up with this girl. In this huge house in Miami, she's like twenty-one, hot as hell . . . So they're all outside the bedroom beating on each other, and I'm inside, fucking this girl for like three hours. Do you like pussy? Cuz I'm gonna turn forty next month, and I'll tell ya, they don't come around like they used to. Nothing like being with one half your age, right? So she starts freaking out, wanting to leave cuz of the commotion, and I say no and grab her by the hand. Outside, there's an ax that's entered the picture, it's crazy. But it turns out she likes it rough, so all they can hear through the door is SLAP SLAP SLAP, me pummeling her ass . . .

"So me and my federal judge pal have a falling-out, and ya know what he can do? Since 9/11 and Homeland Security and shit, he puts me on the list. I can't get on a plane. Didn't used to be that way—I had a DUI in Illinois, so I just got a license in another state, then I went overseas and got an international ID! But now all the agencies are talking to each other, had to go to Group Dynamics therapy, anger management, Cocaine Anonymous, all to get the damn thing back . . . How did I lose it? Well, the cops had it in for me cuz we'd gotten one of 'em fired for a racial beat-down, so they watched me for eighteen months and finally got me. They said to pull over, but I had all kinds of drugs on me, so I figured I'd save $150 on the tow and just drive to the police station. They had *nine* cruisers following me, going thirty miles an hour.

"Finally got back to Chicago, should still be there banging that chick, but what do I do first thing? Back to the bar and drink more tequila . . . I love you guys, you save my life listening to my shit—is this *Taxicab Confessions*? Just kidding, man, you're the best! Take it easy, brother, be safe."

Player of the Game

"Ashland and Cortez. Take me there fast. There's cocaine there."
These are his words before he even sits down. He gets in out of the throng on Clark in the middle of Wrigleyville. His eyes are hidden behind cheap white plastic-rimmed sunglasses shielding him from the glare of night, his chin and cheeks decorated with a hipster's stubble, his red retro T-shirt with "PLAYER OF THE GAME" spelled out in white with ornamental stars completing the design.
"Just being honest. Whatever you think at this time of night, man,

just get me there fast," he says, then, satisfied with my proposed route, he launches into a soliloquy about whether it's a good idea for his friend to cheat on his wife with someone from the office. Then he falls silent.

From time to time, he inquires as to our progress, then sinks back into his openmouthed stupor. "Whoa, this is *really* far south. Where *is* Cortez, anyway?" Having only every fifth question answered or even acknowledged doesn't faze him in the least. We pull up to the address, and he casts an uncertain look toward the condo, then back at me, before paying up and stumbling across the street.

The Difference between North and South

He lists from side to side at a stop sign, raising his arm in my direction. The work it takes him to name his destination should've told me to leave him where he was. After several attempts to understand one another, we finally settle on the Chicago Board of Trade in the Loop. There's a state of inebriation just short of blackout in which random disconnected phrases escape a drunk's mouth, where he is convinced that his friends are still talking to him when, in fact, he's alone in a taxi heading home. He attempts conversation without much success, then begins to grow agitated; he's convinced that I'm taking him the wrong way, trying to rip him off. We're headed southbound on Lakeshore Drive, so I helpfully point at the dark void of the lake to our left, to ease his fears. This unfortunately only serves to enrage him more. He boasts of his great wealth, his condo downtown, and more, to prove that no lousy hack could put one over on him. When this line of reasoning doesn't win the day, he resorts to insults. I won't repeat the long litany save for what he punctuates it all with—

"YOU'RE A FUCKIN' NIGGER!"

I stifle a laugh and don't respond until we reach his address. He apologizes and pays for his fare, then teeters out, still unsure on his feet, headed God knows where.

The Fellas

Four pile in early in the evening. We all know them too well. A few years out of school, just married but before the kids and the inevitable move to the 'burbs; or still playing the field, getting obliterated every weekend. Get them together and the collective IQ might not muster the know-how to change a lightbulb. They call each other only by last name as if they're teammates, but more likely from some vestigial custom of fraternity days. They kid about fucking the girlfriends of buddies who aren't there. As we near the bar, they make their final preparations. Jenson's definitely going to be the wingman, while Jones and Fletcher will hang back, then come in to close the deal. There *better* be some talent at this joint, they all agree.

Stopped at a red, I look to the left. On the sidewalk outside Tavern in Wicker Park, a shirtless man balls his fists, ready to take on all comers. Eyes flit this way and that, muscles flex, then go slack. There's no one within ten feet of him, so, seeing no takers, he picks

up his white T-shirt off the ground and puts it back on. Tucking it in carefully, he gives the street a last once-over and goes back into the bar. The light turns green.

Two men and a woman stumble out of the condo loft building. Whether to go for the left or right door becomes a complicated decision, but they eventually persevere. "Guess I'm sitting bitch," the one in the middle announces to all concerned. They're making two stops (the bitch's being first of course). The fellow by the window is in Mardi Gras beads in the dead of winter. His eyes might as well have *X*'s over them like they do in the old cartoons; he's no longer on this plane. He knows, however, that he wants to keep partying with his pal. The girl will have none of it, informing him in a stern, motherly tone that it's time to go home.

Extricating the "bitch" is accomplished at a glacial pace with phones and crumpled bills dropped and picked up several times. He makes one more attempt to talk her into prolonging the revelry before climbing back in and laying his head on her lap.

At their house, she hands me the fare, accompanied by a look that says that this kind of thing is getting old fast. "C'mon, Jeff, it's time to go home!" she says, and stalks off. There's a glove left on the backseat, and when I hand it to him, he grins and says, "Hey, thass Coleman's glove!" as if discovering a lost toy. He waves it my way, then staggers in the direction in which she disappeared.

Freakeasy

They're in luck. The address I'd been sent to twice didn't yield a soul, so they can stop shivering on that windswept corner and get in. Two girls and two guys, barely into their twenties. Among the couple dozen articles of clothing covering them, no two match. If colors come close, then sizes diverge; a loose furry top paired with the tightest skirt; unkempt scraggly hair and shiny dance shoes; a straw cowboy hat and a green Day-Glo bracelet. They only get to be this young once.

The chick in the cowboy hat sits up front and wants to get to know me better—at the close of the night, it's sometimes tough for them to turn it off. This one will leave a morgue full of victims in her wake before she is through. From batted lashes to a dozen different smiles to the feigned amusement at any and every word, she shows off just a bit of the repertoire. "We were at the Freakeasy tonight," she says.

A loft in an industrial stretch of the city, a DJ, a light show, dancing, drugs; in other words, a rave. "No," the bearded kid in the back

insists. "Well, sort of, but more sophisticated, you know, because they're way beyond *that* . . . If you're not into a bunch of hot bitches shaking their asses all night, then I don't recommend it," he snickers. "There's like a bunk bed above the DJ booth and they've taken out the mattresses and it's like a chill-out area," the chick chimes in. There's knowing references to various illicit substances and giggling.

"Not that we do any of that," someone in back reassures me. "Gotta be super careful, man, especially in Chicago . . ."

Every succeeding generation discovers much the same vices and acts as if they're the first. These kids are hardly out on their own, and it's vital for them to let the world know how far out they are. I ask the girl why they're going home so early—only 3 a.m., after all—and she says, "My lady love back there has an early morning thing she's gotta do and we live in BuFu, Egypt, so . . ." Asking where this Bumfuck, Egypt, is situated reveals it to be Dyer, Indiana, about a forty-five-minute drive out of the city.

"You should go back to the Freakeasy, man. It was like $20 to get in, but they probably won't charge you. Just like tell 'em you're there to pick someone up. They'll be going till the sun comes up." She pays up with a collection of sweaty bills, flashes a dazed grin, then follows her friends out of the cab. The rest of the journey to BuFu apparently will be completed by some other mode of transport.

Marriage

She dwarfs him by a good foot or so, yet he steers her down the steps and into the backseat with practiced efficiency. "She's going to 22nd Place and Western," he says, looking hard at me to be sure that she is delivered there safely.

"Where are we?" she asks, looking out the window at the deserted early morning street. Being reassured of our location seems to ease her mind a bit, though a few minutes later she wonders how long it'll be until she's home. "He wanted me to spend the night, but I gotta go to church in the morning. He always does. He don't understand—I have no one except my pastor. If I don't come, he'll wonder what's wrong, and the next time he'll lecture me.

"I'm so sorry. I've been drinking, and you don't wanna do this . . . He told me that if I get in the cab and leave, it's over." Nearing her house, she repeats these things until the tears begin to flow, and in front of the gate it's clear the burden has not yet been lifted; the engine idles and she keeps asking questions to which I have no answers.

"I want to marry him so much, but he won't go into the church, doesn't believe in it. What can I do? . . . You don't know me and don't care about me and this shit, so what do you think I should do? Thank you so much for taking me home, I know you didn't want to." Her tearstained face is right up to the open partition, darkly lacquered nails reflecting the streetlights as her hand rests on the runner of the sliding window, threatening the established distance needed to convey customers to their desired destinations without being dragged along in their wake. Without that barrier, the line can be blurred further than the typical alcohol-aided intimacy of a Saturday night.

"I love him, but he won't agree to it. The church is all I got. I'll wake up in two hours and go . . . Will you please wait until I get inside my house?"

She balances one uncertain foot after the other through the metal gate, then to the door and in, waving her hand and disappearing into the unlit house.

SUNDAY

The dregs of Saturday night will often spill into Sunday, but by late morning the pace slackens to a leisurely gait. Even the most determined ragers need to sleep it off eventually. Many cabdrivers, too, choose this as their day of rest. Thus, there's less competition, so it's possible to profit without getting too much gray hair. Sunday is also the day for those who work weekends to let loose, so people-watching opportunities still abound.

Nite Cap

It's nearing three o'clock on a Sunday morning, the hour at which bars disgorge their more dedicated patrons. I'm going eastbound on Irving in Portage Park, when a round-faced woman runs out from the Nite Cap calling, "I've got one more inside, will you wait please?" I turn on the meter and wait. The marquee above the door advertises

a week's worth of heavy metal cover bands. She comes back out with a blond version of herself in tow. "I can't believe I got a cab this quick out here, thought for sure we'd be stranded for hours," she says. "You're our hero!"

They're probably in their early forties, dolled up for a night out, with makeup showing the strain of many hours' wear. The brunette gives a Roscoe Village address, and we shove off. I hop on the Kennedy to skip a few traffic lights, and when we exit on Addison, they ask if we can stop at the White Castle on the corner of Kedzie.

The drive-thru queue wraps around the white-parapeted shack. Undaunted, the ladies pass the time recapping their evening. The blonde apparently had been making out with one of the longhairs inside the Nite Cap when her friend dragged her out to the cab. "He was kinda cute, right? I wrote my number across his whole forearm. He said he was still going out, so maybe he'll call later." The brunette laughs and asks me my name. "We're eighties rock chicks, you could tell, right? You know, we like those metal dudes." The line inches forward, and they bitch about what a fortune this cab ride is turning out to cost.

Our turn comes, and the blonde launches into her order without any bidding. Her friend squeals for her to shut up. She asks if I want some burgers, and when I say, "Not these," she concedes that nobody really wants them and that they'd be paying for this decision before morning broke. Finally prompted by the feedback-laden squawk from the speaker, the blonde recites a list that includes sliders, fries, chicken rings, fish nibblers, and half a dozen other items, racking up a $25 bill—which at White Castle is quite an impressive amount for two.

The rundown of their night continues as we inch toward the window. "We're not on *Taxicab Confessions*, are we?" one of them asks. When it was time to pay, the blonde reads the credit card swipe instructions out loud: " 'Slide in and out quickly!' That's what she said! Ha-ha-ha-ha-ha-ha!" Her friend asks me how sick of them I am by now. They both try, with little success, to chat up the kid with the headset in the window.

Fast-food smells permeate the cab as we pull back out onto Addison. They grow quiet, rustling wrappers, unable to hold off until home, hunger replacing lust. On the brunette's street, we turn south and stop just past the second speed bump. They stumble out, leaving a trail of wax-paper wrappers in their wake. And so their Saturday night ends with no prince despite a trip to the Castle.

Modesty

Five a.m. and the two of them are the last outside the bar's locked doors. "Your place?" he asks her as they get in, and the Lincoln Park address she offers makes him ask, "You live there?"

Whether they'd met at the last watering hole or at the one just before that, they make an odd pair. She's made up and wears clothes that obviously set her back something, whereas he's a scrawny bespectacled hipster type. The need to warm another's bed has bridged the class and cultural chasm once more.

"I get it," she says. "Ever since I got to this town, the guys I've dated have been infatuated with who I am." Eliciting no more than a murmured assent, she continues, "I've always been the best at anything I've ever tried. *Oh yeah*, I was the Homecoming Queen . . . I'm

passionate about everything I do; my sisters were model-gorgeous, in beauty contests, so I'm all about competing and getting what I want."

All through her speech, he cowers closer and closer to the window, present in body but edging toward flight. As we pull into the high-rise's drive, he leaves without a word and loiters uncertainly by the glass doors. "My little boyfriend here is allergic to paying his way. A real winner!" she announces, digging the MasterCard from her purse. She bolts inside, high-fiving the doorman; he follows sheepishly in her wake.

Soldier

A little after 5 a.m. Sunday morning and the line for the cashier at the garage stretches all the way back to the pool table. This is a disaster. Fourteen hours driving and this is the reward? She's the one that double- and triple-counts every nickel too, so I decide to go back out and try to squeeze one last dollar out of the night. Heading toward the nearest late-night bar to see if any tardy revelers are orphaned

and in need of assistance, he waves me down. A clean-cut guy in a pea coat, his only request is to smoke; his destination is the farthest northwestern reaches of the city. He gets on the phone.

". . . ready for Wednesday? I've been keeping in pretty good shape, running every day except yesterday. Went out last night, oof . . . Just hope it's not like my third deployment, it's gonna be rough . . . Yeah, somewhere outside Kabul . . . Huh? Man, no, he's out of his mind, he started some shit with these navy guys two weeks back, went absolutely berserk. Totally unfit, can't believe they're letting him back in . . . His plan is to go to Haiti, but that ain't gonna happen, I *hope* they send him there because he won't take orders, he's just gonna go in and FUCK SHIT UP.

"My mom's not doing so well, doubt she'll make it more than a few months. Once she really starts going downhill, she'll fade fast. I'll have to come home, not gonna be in some foreign rat-hole when my mother's dying . . . Dad's having a hard time. She can still do the everyday little things, but she can't handle the big stuff. She calls for help; he's losing his mind.

"No, that's not going well, it's pretty much over. She's just about done. She isn't about to commit to being single for one more year. It's understandable—I don't blame her. We had a pretty bad fight about it . . .

"You know, they'll have me running point the way they like, going into booby-trapped caves with folks that don't like us. It's gonna be bad . . . *No*, I'm not working with the ___ Airborne again, they really fucked us last time. We were running intel for them, then we hear these blasts, and they just mow down like fifty women and children. We *never* ordered an air strike! Not a civilian male anywhere in sight, and those psychos are celebrating. They just murdered fifty innocents and they're proud—what a clusterfuck . . . You know what happened in Fallujah, right? . . . No, that's the story we told, but . . . so, he's searching the guy and he's already given up his weapons, his knife, his AK are laying down, he's searching him and everything's normal, then I look over and he just snaps his neck. The guy's partner sees this and I can tell he's about to start freaking out, so I go over and slash his throat to just shut him up . . . Bad shit, he won't listen to his COs. He should've been court-martialed, but he's going back in instead . . . I got a bad feeling the way the things are going over there. Should've gotten whacked two or three times over. Always get a bad feeling at the start of these. Bags are packed, HOO-HA, it's GO TIME! . . . Okay, man, I'll see ya Wednesday . . ."

There's silence and he makes no mention of his conversation, just pays and gets out. I watch him in the rearview mirror just standing and staring at the house, lighting another cigarette, not anxious to go in.

Back at the garage, the line's barely moved. Outside dawn is breaking and the soldier's story lingers.

Good Omen

The old man stands on the corner, looking this way and that, a hand cart holding a cardboard box marked EGGS, waiting expectantly at the curb. The cab is parked just beyond him, and as I pass, he points at it and asks, "Is that you?"

We load the cart carefully into the trunk, the contents of the box covered by cloth, heavy enough to require both our efforts. His destination is within a block of the restaurant I'd decided on for my breakfast. "I'm your first fare, maybe I bring you luck," he says.

He'd been waiting out there for the Western bus, but it had seemingly been rerouted because of the Mexican parade. He's as grateful for the ride as I'm surprised to have someone pay the cost of my breakfast so soon after leaving the house. As a rule, people in my neighborhood don't take cabs; they wait for the bus without giving the taxi a second glance. It's understandable, as I rarely take cabs myself—it's a luxury that many of us cannot afford regularly. I usually drive miles before I spot the first upraised hand and the meter clicks to life.

We sail north on Western in contented silence, quick glances in the rearview mirror revealing a healthy crop of graying nose hairs but an otherwise placid countenance; both of us are occupied by our own ruminations. His day's labors apparently at an end, mine only just beginning.

As I pull over at the corner of Augusta, he pays and asks for assistance with his cargo. The contents shifted a bit as the box was lifted out—food or perhaps something else to be sold on some corner

where people pass by, yet remaining mysterious and unnamed. He refastens the straps holding the whole thing together, thanks me, and wheels it away down the sidewalk. I park the cab, buy the Sunday paper from the BP gas station, and go toward the café to put his $10 toward the cost of an omelet and some coffee.

Worker

Stopped at a red on a quiet Sunday night. The kid in the bulky sweatshirt and spiked hair stands waiting at the bus stop, peeking through the cab's window tentatively before reaching out a palm to ascertain whether it's available. "Thanks, man. Cold as shit out there. Was nice and sunny, then six o'clock hit and it dropped like a motherfucker . . . See, I was hangin' with my girl, and she's the kind that likes to go walk outside after a meal. Course she didn't bring no sweater, so I gave 'er mine and near froze my ass off."

He wants to know if the Bears won and, hearing that they did, explains about how his friend knows this site where you can watch all the fights and games for free. "He's got it hooked up to his plasma, it's all hi-def, and you don't have to pay nothin'." He wants to know how late my shift runs. "Wow, that's so late, and I bitch about my hours. Gotta be there 4 a.m. and stay till 10."

He takes care of the lawns of repo'd houses. "It's easy, we just go in there with a weed-whacker—one, two, three, we're done. There's like seventy-two in Chicago, then a shitload more in the 'burbs. They're adding more all the time." He got the job because his uncle, who ran a fence company, was asked by a real estate pal if he knew anyone who could help with the maintenance of all the seized property piling up on his plate. Recognizing a payday when he saw it, he brought the nephews and cousins in to share a piece of the action. "It's all right, I guess. I applied at that new La Quinta Inn Downtown; there were like thousands waiting. I was there six hours, but I thought it'd work out cuz I had an in. I was gonna be a mini-bar attendant, $13 an hour, but they wouldn't give it to me since I ain't twenty-one."

He is just out of high school and the only one of his friends with a steady job. "I'd rather be working. They have side jobs, this and that, but it's mostly just hangin' around." He wants to keep talking, but we're at his house, so he pays up and darts out. There's always more, but the story hardly ever continues past the allotted time, the length of the ride is all that's offered. Often, though, it's more than enough to get a glimpse into another's world.

On Tap

The fat disheveled man gropes the girl with his left hand, his right raised toward the street, the whole scene lit by the Old Style sign overhead.

Giving her one last squeeze, he guides her into the cab, then blows a kiss in farewell and goes into the bar. She doesn't look back at him. "Austin and Roosevelt, but pull around the corner where he can't see. Should take my ass home, but sometimes the devil gets in you," she tells me. She has me pull over and gets on her cell, cooing,

"Where you at, baby? You still partying downtown? Yeah, just got done with my date . . . Oh, all right. I'll jus' go home, then." She lets the disappointment sink in for a moment, then tells me to head toward the highway.

A glance or two in the rearview mirror registers a woman in her late twenties or early thirties. The elaborate eyeliner, tight-fitting geometrically printed dress, and long straightened hair worn up with a kerchief in a matching pattern gives her a '50s look. The slob at the bar back there must have paid a good chunk of his paycheck for her company. She tells me that she's staying with two gay guys out in Berwyn after wrecking her place. "They make me call when I'm on my way home so they can let me in. They don't trust me with my own keys, and I don't blame them. They're all right . . . It's only ten o'clock so I should be OK."

We speed west on the Eisenhower in silence, thinking our own thoughts. Does she regularly meet up with grubby old men at crummy bars, or is this reserved for quiet Sunday evenings when no better prospects present themselves? There's no polite way to broach such a subject, so I content myself with speculating. I recognize this silence of hers, however—it's the same as the stripper's en route to the club, the quiet time spent girding herself for what she has to do to get by another day.

Off the expressway and south on Austin Boulevard, past Roosevelt, we turn onto a side street lined with bungalows. She points out the one to stop at, then hands $25 through the open partition. She thanks me and puts out her hand, zeroing in with her cold dark eyes and telling me her name. Is she trying to line up another date? No way of knowing, but this must be how it's done. I wish her a good night, and she walks up the gangway between two nearly identical little brick houses and out of sight as I pull away, uncertain what's on tap.

Gandalf

I've been off a few weeks. Coming back to the garage to get a cab late on a Sunday night is no cause for celebration, but there was no way of knowing what hell was in store. Judging by the cashier's face, it's clear that it doesn't look good.

Normally putting your name on the waiting list before midnight on a Sunday or Monday will give you a fair chance of getting out of there a few hours later with some sort of vehicle. The list is capped at ten, so if you're eleventh, you come back and try again the next day. That night there were seventy names in line. Another cab company had gotten into some kind of trouble with the city, and a bunch of their cabs were pulled off the street. This forced their drivers to seek cars elsewhere, bringing us to the present situation. The sympathetic cashier takes down my chauffeur's license and cell phone number, suggesting I come back the next afternoon but not leaving much cause for optimism.

I come back the following day and the night after that to no avail. By Wednesday or Thursday on a typical week (much less a disaster of one than this week), there's not much chance of landing anything, so figuring to try again Sunday, I write the week off. The plan is to go in around midnight and sit there until something turns up. In preparation for this, I'm at my favorite bar drinking bourbon early Saturday evening when my phone rings. They have a cab for me, but I have to pick it up in the next hour or it will go to the next guy in the queue. Leaving my friends with the promise of a quick return, I hightail it to the garage.

It's a real beater—five years old, 323,000 miles, with every attendant wheeze, squeak, and groan. The driver's side door locks on its own when not held open, the meter is missing buttons—I'd need to jab at a taped-over cavity to start the thing—but this and myriad other defects have to be ignored as the prospect of more days off would begin to seriously make keeping a roof overhead a dicey proposition. I speed back to the bar to toast my good fortune.

The next day, attempting to log in to the computerized taxi dispatch system, another problem with my chariot rears its head. The whole setup is called a Gandalf. It replaced the two-way radio of old with the grizzled dispatcher squawking day and night, causing every shift to be accompanied by a low-grade migraine. The little screen displays the available fares with little backtalk and few recriminations. For the seven years that I've used it, the procedure has been the same—sign in with your company code, and you're good to go, happy hunting. Well, this Sunday morning it doesn't work. Putting in the code repeatedly yields a message to "SWIPE THE CARD." The meter is locked and useless without being logged into the system, so there's no use in driving at this point. Having never seen this before and not knowing what else to do, I go back to the garage to have it looked at.

On Sundays at the cab barn only a skeleton crew shows up. It's a 24-hours-a-day/7-days-a-week industry, but you wouldn't know it by the hours that the mechanics and management keep. Telling the shop guy my problem, he tells me there's no one to look into it just now. I have to drop the cab and go back home and wait for them to call whenever it's repaired or another vehicle becomes available. Standing in line to hand over the meter to the cashier, another driver asks if he can take the roll of meter paper out of mine as he'd run out. Not thinking anything of it, I hand it over.

By 8 p.m., figuring there'd be nothing happening this night, I settle in for the evening with a movie and a heated-up can of soup. The phone rings: it's the night manager saying my cab is fixed. Telling him that I wasn't able to log into the system came as a surprise. "That what was wrong? Well, it'll be fixed by the time you get here," he promises. Makes me wonder what it was they had "fixed" in the intervening eight hours. The old-timer who drives me over listens to my story and informs me that the procedure has changed—we now have to swipe our Yellow Cab Company ID cards in lieu of punching in the code for access. This means that there's nothing wrong with my jalopy's Gandalf, and I get to feel like an idiot to boot.

The nearly toothless night manager greets me by more or less accusing me of tampering with the meter. "Ain't nothing wrong with it. Won't work with the buttons missing and no paper in it," he crows. It takes all the reserves of self-control I can summon not to smack the old fool in the face. The policy is to compensate the time lost with a shop credit. This hardly makes up for a day of fares as the formula is just to divide up the cost of the lease—it works out to $3 and change per hour; my eight hours is good for about $25. Now that it is determined that there is nothing wrong, I won't even get that. I'm pretty steamed by the time it's my turn at the cashier's window. Treating the poor guy on the other side of the glass with a barrage of curses aimed at the night manager, I sign my lease and am about to hand over the full payment when he stops me short. "No, look, he gave you six hours credit," he says, beaming. For once incompetence and inconsistency work out in my favor.

Instead of having another go at the dentally challenged creep, I tear out of there, content to steer the creaky old Crown Vic through the streets the best I can. The lost day could have easily been avoided with some simple explanation, but that would have made common sense and that is just not how we do it in the cab industry.

HOLIDAY

Working holidays in the cab is a special kind of lonesome. Not much will make you feel more left out than when the whole world is celebrating while you work. The dining options also leave a lot to be desired. On the other hand, there are few better occasions to watch people as they attempt to enjoy themselves. That's what we're supposed to do on the holidays.

Stanley Cup

The afternoon before the Chicago Blackhawks won the 2010 Stanley Cup started as most any Wednesday would. Around 3 p.m. the early birds of the office flock tiptoe toward the streets and homeward, occasionally catching a cab to hasten their flight. The avenues begin to thicken and clog with the start of the evening exodus. A blonde in her twenties asks to go to one of the taverns on Madison a few blocks east of the United Center. "It's not even 4 p.m., so it shouldn't be too bad at West End, right?" she asks. We can see the line of jersey-clad fans circling the building from two blocks away. "Oh no . . . just drop me here, I guess, don't know where to go now."

Bars in every neighborhood fill their sidewalk seats to overflowing with red-white-and-black-attired revelers. Most eyes are glued to the flat screens broadcasting the big game; other people are swept along in the overall enthusiasm of the crowd. Driving past with no horse in the race, nothing riding on the outcome, I'm free to take it all in at

face value. The yelps and whoops escaping from so many windows
foreshadow the roars to come hours later. So many different-shaped
bodies in uniform puts one in mind of a poorly trained militia with
leaderless splinter cells roaming the side streets on mystery missions.
Working on this night, as with so many other festive nights, sets one
necessarily apart from the masses. Climbing onto the bandwagon at
this point would've been ludicrous in any case. Hockey just doesn't
do a thing for me.

When the Blackhawks finally win it sometime after 10 p.m., the volume of the night goes up to eleven and stays there for hours. From horns blaring to caterwauling celebrators to improvised explosives, my low-grade headache graduates to full-blown migraine in minutes. On Ontario east of Michigan Avenue, Chicago's Finest would have made Old Man Daley beam the way they're preserving the disorder. With cruisers parked perpendicular to create more of a bottleneck than the surging masses manage on their own, the men in blue stick out their chests and peer this way and that. Clearing their gauntlet somehow, I turn south onto Michigan and pick up a pretty girl in a green summer dress. "How about those Hawks!" is what I think she says, though the ringing in my ears makes most speech the barest whisper.

Two women run into the middle of Randolph in the West Loop and ask to be taken north. "We were at Market and they wouldn't even let us turn the TVs up! Can you believe that shit? . . . That place is full of douche-bags anyways. Most of them didn't even turn their heads to watch. Take us someplace where we can do it up right!" The farther north we go on Halsted, the thicker the crowds became, many reaching in to slap hands and holler at every passing vehicle.

The car horns continue to blare, punctuated occasionally by more piercing reports from distant quarters. Coming up to Fullerton and Western, a plume of smoke rises and spreads over the entire intersection as Streets and San men shovel sand to douse a trash bin set ablaze. Many overcome costumed zealots have to be dodged with deft maneuvers as they seem no longer to accept the sidewalks as their natural habitat. The migraine mutates and throbs in heretofore unknown sectors of my cranium. The *GO, HAWKS!* screams go on and on, despite the fact that they've gone as far as there is to go.

Near 2 a.m. it's time to call it a night, but not before picking up a couple who say they'd be paying by debit card before ducking out of sight and proceeding to have at each other in the most desperate way. With the ride being barely a mile in duration, their amazing ardor could only get them so far; fixing their clothes back into place as best they can, they stumble out to continue marking the home team's big night behind closed doors.

Fourth of July

It is the local custom to mark our nation's birth by staking out spots by the waterfront. People fight for the best places, the parking lots along the beach full-up by midmorning. Waves of half-dressed patriots rush eastward to roast in the July sun, to be closer to the nighttime fireworks display marking the Fourth. Much of the afternoon is taken up with trips to the North, Belmont, Montrose, Foster, and other beaches. Or as close to them as the police blockades would allow, as the crowds swelled with each passing hour; families would jump out and unload folding chairs, grills, charcoal, and umbrellas from the taxi's trunk in the middle of Lake Shore Drive on-ramps and hurdle over and around barriers toward the lake. There's something primal about these throngs drawing toward water as so many, at one time or another, long to be back near the sea.

At the corner of McClurg and Ontario, a barefoot man, furiously sucking on a cigarette, flags me down. "Take me to Schaumburg?" he asks in a short way.

"Sure," I answer—who'd turn down an $85 fare? We make our way west to the Kennedy without any chatter except for the permission given to keep smoking. Then he gets on his cell. "What do you mean, where am I? I'm in a cab going to Schaumburg . . . YOU told me to get out of the car! YOU did your fake act being a tough guy, what did you expect me to do? I'm taking a fuckin' $150 cab ride because of you!?!" He hangs up and lights another. Some ten miles and several calls later, he asks to be taken to Navy Pier instead.

The crush of buses, taxis, trolleys, and all other manner of conveyance as we near is close to impenetrable, but all the while he's describing what he sees out the window, triangulating his friends' exact location. "I'm directly across from, like, a gigantic hot air balloon. Where are you?" They're going to pay his $40-and-climbing cab fare as some sort of peace offering. Idling in front of the Pier's main entrance for some ten minutes, enduring dirty looks from the traffic aides and rent-a-cops recruited to assist on the holiday, a girl finally comes up and hands her MasterCard through the passenger's side window. "Where the hell did you go?" she asks, signing the slip, though it's unclear whether her question is directed at him or at me.

The explosions increase as night begins to fall. Dogs lose bladder control and hide under beds this time of year, and some of us who walk upright don't feel much better. The tumult and flashing lights do nothing for my equilibrium, and a few hours into it, a corkscrew begins to work at two or three strategic points inside my skull, affecting my mood adversely. Somewhere on Sheridan Road, an old man gets the full brunt for his inability to keep that boat of a Lincoln in his own lane—when I suggest that he'd be better served taking a trolley or a golf cart, his grown son in the passenger's seat takes exception and suggests that I relax and mind my own business. One thing for sure: I wouldn't be caught dead out here if there wasn't money at stake. The fact that the masses submit to it of their own volition makes me question my membership in the species.

Stuck behind a booze bus on Clark Street, a guy with slicked-back hair hangs out of the back window trying to get my fare's attention. He jabs a little flag in her direction and roars, "LADY, AMERICA!!! YEAH!?!" and slams his beer.

At 9:30 p.m., with the lakefront display seemingly over, an exodus of sunburned bodies trudges west. Three luck out and get to the taxi on Fullerton, and we get on Lake Shore northbound. Halfway to the Belmont exit, traffic comes to a standstill in the center and right lanes. Thinking the ramp's backed up, I veer into the left lane only to see the sky ignited once more with multicolored flares and notice that all those vehicles have their hazards on as their occupants are mesmerized by the light show over the harbor. I drive on as my passengers *ooh* and *aah* out the window, happy for the encore performance. An hour or two more of hauling the lakefront revelers saps the last of my strength.

A rye on the rocks at a friend's quiet bar serves to put the day's cacophony to rest before hanging it up for the night. What blowing shit up has to do with our independence must be left to more nimble minds, though parking the cab at 2 a.m., the sparklers seen going full bore down the street prove that my neighbors' ardor for America shows no sign of abating.

Halloween

The kiddie candy-gathering aspect of Halloween is eclipsed by the nocturnal masked bacchanal more with each passing year. The packs of chaperoned, orderly children hauling pumpkin-hued plastic bags of sweets disappear with the setting sun, to be replaced by more or less creatively disguised hordes.

This year, to add to the high jinks, daylight saving time ends on the same night, adding an extra hour of imbibing to the delight of the reveling masses as the clock falls back, making 2 a.m. 1 a.m. again. No chauffeur of any standing would pass on it. Nevertheless, after a time, the marauding crowds spilling from all directions make for a chaotic and exhausting work environment; we truly earn it on these nights.

There is no shortage of funny getups—Forrest Gump giving me chocolates and debating the dubious merits of the film that spawned him; two pretty girls dressed as Tweedle Dee and Tweedle Dum; half a dozen mostly mediocre Fred Flintstones; a guy in a very professionally constructed Whoopee Cushion costume.

The girl I pick up on a radio call at around the second 2 a.m. (the

one that was really 3 a.m.) doesn't stand out for what she wears but more for what she says. She's in a short black dress, fishnets, with very red lipstick and nails. Plopping in the backseat, she immediately asks whether it's OK to smoke, then if she can sit up front. This is normally a big no-no—unless there's no room in the back, no one sits in the passenger seat. Besides the possible safety concerns, it implies a familiarity that few drivers would welcome when confronted with the average passenger. These are not our friends, we aren't giving them a lift, and no matter how casually we're often addressed, this is still a business transaction. For whatever reason, I let that all go.

"Thank you for taking me home." She smiles, a bit bleary-eyed. "So I invited him to a slumber party, and he turned me down. I said, 'Wanna come over for a sleepover, just you and me?' and he said no . . . What's up with that?" In response to the less-than-comforting clichés I offer, she isn't impressed. "You don't know me; I'm not that kind of girl. This is the one for me. He's only thirty and a partner in a law firm. He's everything I ever wanted. I'm straight-up small-town. I just wanna be taken care of, you know? He opens doors for me—it makes all the difference."

She'd been at a girlfriend's party texting her dream guy, making arrangements, and when it didn't turn out as she'd hoped, she was in no mood to celebrate any longer. "Anyways, she's moving to Mexico ON MY BIRTHDAY! So fuck her . . . So, what about you?" She refuses to believe that her driver has no personal life, but unable to glean any details, she lets it go to blow clouds of smoke out the window.

"I can tell you're a decent guy or I wouldn't have sat up front," she says as we slow at her doorstep. "Will you give me a hug?"

I do.

November 4, 2008

Eastbound on Roosevelt around 8:30 p.m., approaching the southwest corner of Grant Park, swarms collect slowly drifting north; the left onto Michigan Avenue takes three green lights. The crowd swells, threatening the path of cars and buses, oblivious, otherwise occupied. Tchotchkes are hawked at every opportunity, from the Dollar Store to haute couture in service to the cause.

My passengers hop out at the far end of the park, and I head away from the throngs, back to the neighborhoods, with the idea of shepherding more pilgrims to the altar. At Damen and Division, a white '75 Caprice guns a left, causing the bumper of my cab to make close acquaintance with its right rear quarter panel, effectively ending my night. He attempts to slip away but is thwarted a mere half block down by a police cruiser.

At the garage, photos of the damage are taken, then the wait begins. The TV in the waiting room blares out the election results; the trickle of drivers react ecstatically, bursting with a nearly familial pride; many believing their shared African heritage with the president-elect entitle them to some small share of the victory. As the hours drag on, having seen the speeches, analysis, maps, charts, and interviews dozens of times, one impression lingers: This one really was different. Contrary to the fanatic zeal and adoration of his acolytes, Obama seems as close to a real person as we've seen in the last twenty years of presidential hopefuls. It would be good not to feel ashamed or disgusted to be a citizen of this country; if nothing else, it'll be refreshing to have a leader who can form a complete sentence.

Fourteen hours and fifteen cigarettes later, I finally get a cab. Rolling out, the sun stings my sleep-deprived eyes, despite which a tentative hopeful feeling attempts to gain purchase.

Thanksgiving

I'm on my way to a traditional Thanksgiving meal of pot stickers and spicy pan-fried pork at Lao Sze Chuan when he flags me down on Roosevelt. A young guy in a track suit and expensive basketball shoes. The first words out of his mouth are about how his car has broken down, which to anyone who's lived in the city means a scam or just plain panhandling. In the spirit of the day, I don't object and he directs me to an address on the South Side.

He tells me about going to an event with Chicago Bulls players, proudly showing the autographs he's collected. He's excited like a kid would be, leading me to think that perhaps the broken-down car might actually exist. His innocence and lack of guile makes me doubt that I'm being played. He asks if I'd had my Thanksgiving meal.

When we get to his house, he tells me that his mother will have the $25 for the cab. He has me honk a few times, then goes into the yard and hollers up at the second-floor window. Eventually a dark form appears and a complicated negotiation begins. I can only make out what my passenger is saying—it amounts to pleading and promising to pay back the amount in question. It goes on for close to fifteen minutes, with the figure in the window grudgingly tossing a crumpled bill out past the overgrown shrubbery of the yard. He comes up to the driver's side, sheepishly offering a $20 bill. "It's all she has."

He says his name is Dwayne and shakes my hand when I accept it.

Christmas

The abandoned streets that one's accustomed to at 4 a.m. are odd, eerie, and lonesome at 4 p.m. on a Christmas Day. The few wandering souls who stand out are the kind who would fade into the scenery on a typical day. The absence of others brings them into higher

relief, into sharper focus than they warrant or than anyone would ever want them to be in. The unkempt man talking to the brick wall to the side of a shuttered storefront might not catch the eye with a stream of pedestrians ignoring him, but today he's the only show in town.

The few who require transport seem more in their own worlds than on other days. Maybe it's the long pauses between encountering anyone, but these rides feel like incursions into foreign lands; care must be taken not to antagonize the natives or break local customs while backtracking out and away from them.

Two teenage girls preface every direction and request with *sir*, making me wonder whether it's an ironic game or whether they were raised with some stilted out-of-date formality and this was the one day of the year that their families allowed them to go out among the commoners.

A young, well-dressed Asian woman hefting a mountain of gifts hails me in a tony neighborhood. She asks to be taken to a black ghetto area. There's no chatter during the trip, and upon arrival she hurries out, shielding her face as if she doesn't want to be seen going where she's going.

Much of the day the rain beats down, making the streets appear even emptier than they do already with the dormant vehicles and unpeopled sidewalks, but toward evening it finally begins to form into flakes, to whiten the city and shrink visibility to but a few hundred feet in any direction. I head out to O'Hare in the hope of catching a stray weary traveler or two, to maybe find a hot meal as well.

The little restaurant at the taxi staging area is miraculously open, so Christmas dinner is a fairly tough couple skewers of beef kebab over an ocean of rice with a side of wilted lettuce. The option to drown this last in ranch dressing proves too tempting to resist. The steam rising from the Styrofoam container fogs the car's windows along with the visible breath in the cold, making the surrounding cabs and the airplanes beyond the fence, already being blanketed in snow, fade further and further from view . . . After several hours' wait, kept company by a radio rendition of *It's a Wonderful Life*, it's time to head to the terminals.

The little round-faced man stomps around, finishing his cigarette, near the head of the line at American Airlines. He crawls in and asks to be taken to Hoffman Estates. I look in the book for directions and an estimate on the fare. In an indeterminate Central European accent, he asks incredulously, "They no allow GPS? I trucker and without this I'm lost . . ." I explain of how little use that system is to a city driver, and we shove off westward. Turning into his cookie-cutter subdivision, I start clicking the Extras button on the meter, explaining that we charge the meter plus one half to go out to the suburbs. This prompts the following bit of Old World wisdom from my passenger: "Rules. Too much fucking rules this country. I from Europe . . . I go boating. No drinking, no make noise, go bed ten o'clock. Why I go out, then? Crazy living this country, everyone always chase money . . . Akhhh, glad be home anyway!" He pays $2 above the required $53 and bids me farewell.

Back in the city, a woman stands shivering, clutching a white toy poodle close while trying to hold on to a bunch of sloppily over-stuffed bags. She thanks me profusely for stopping despite the dog. "Most of you guys won't stop when you see him," she says, though how anyone could feel threatened or put off by that little puffball is beyond confounding. Seems her boyfriend chose to celebrate the birth of Jesus by getting lit and smacking her around. She points to the cop cars clustered down the street. "We were having a good time. All I asked him to do was to stop drinking." She's headed to her office to spend the night on the couch. "Luckily my business has one." Still in shock, she thanks me profusely and overtips extravagantly as if to regain some control over a situation that's knocked her on her ass with no warning whatsoever. Driving away, I think no apology for the human race would suffice to make this thing right.

Many hours later, toward dawn, a woman in an oversize parka in the middle of the road is the last fare of the night. She asks about my Christmas, tells about eating way too much and getting most of what she'd asked for this year. We pull up to a house, and she says to wait while she runs in and grabs her kids before disappearing through the gate, down a gangway, and into the dark. Ten minutes later it's time to cut losses. The $10 isn't worth the bother. Maybe Santa had one last gift for her after all.

The holidays magnify all that one lacks, forcing one to brood over deficiencies and failures. The best thing is that they end and everyday life resumes, giving the world back the scale and focus necessary to keep getting by. And me, I'm a stranger among strangers providing some small comfort missing when those others gather behind closed doors for their celebrations.

New Year's Eve

No one threw up in the cab. In other words, my most fervent New Year's wish had been granted. An indication of a fairly restrained evening. The hordes went about their celebrating with workman-like efficiency; collecting fares did not present any special challenge or above-and-beyond effort, every last rider remembering where he or she lived with a bit of encouragement, no unwelcome advances nor invitations to tussle.

The first fare of the afternoon is a couple just approaching the precipice of their sunset years, who might've been the last two theatergoers in the United States not to have seen the Blue Man Group.

He inquires as to what the *Poncho Section* refers to on their tickets; unfortunately their driver is of little help, speculating that something might be hurled their way off the stage. "WELL, we'll be changing seats, then!" the outraged gent announces, remarking also that he didn't realize the theater was "all the way on the North Side." Out-of-towners that feign familiarity with the local geography are always a rare pleasure, but, as they tip generously, no more words should be spent tainting their memory.

Gridlock makes much of the waning daylight a trial as the whole world seems intent on getting to where they are going all at once. The passengers do not complain, no doubt girding themselves for the festivities to come. Bartenders and waitresses on their way in exchange words of encouragement for the slog ahead. We know that many who would cross our paths tonight will be unaccustomed to being out in public, choosing this one night of the year to grace the world with their presence, and thus will demand a special sort of patience of anyone lucky enough to be on the clock.

Just as boredom is setting in, *she* shows up. Mincing steps on high heels to avoid the slick patches bring her to the cab. She introduces herself by name and also, to break the ice, says, "Not to brag on myself, but I just love to love, and the way the world is these days, they just take and take and take." She's thirty-five and on her way to meet a much younger man (this last part confided in a sort of stage whisper). A stop at the liquor store for champagne and then a cigarette lit just as we pull up to the spot. "Shit, can you go around the block? He doesn't know I smoke, and I really need it to get through this." We idle around the corner, where she puffs away, expounding on Obama, online dating, and God knows what else. She was the kind to use your name and make lots of eye contact, leaving the impression that said techniques are being employed to gain advantage. "I hope you get everything you ever wanted in life," she wishes, then crosses the street.

A loud white girl with two Middle Eastern guys in tow is next. "Can't believe that bitch threw a drink at you!" she shrieks to one of her companions. "What kind of party is it when you can't even have a drink? They were all lesbians; she had like a Mohawk and taped-up tits. Bet she'd've been happy if you'd mistaken her for a man." The guys answer meekly, confessing that they just want to get something to eat. It is 11:45 p.m. and they make it to the bar just in time to toast the New Year.

Soon the streets fill with marauding packs, arms raised, leaping into the road in search of transport and bellowing louder as cabs pass, as if their unique call might do the trick where others have failed. Doors locked, zigzagging maneuvers have to be implemented to avoid the enraged gallivanters. Parked outside a pub, many try the doors, walking away suspiciously when it is explained to them that the taxi is reserved. A big shot tries to outbid the rest, offering $20, then $40, to go mere blocks. He stalks away, incredulous that this tactic doesn't produce results, likely reducing his standing in his date's eyes.

Two girls discuss their night: "He was *sooo* short. He plays tennis professionally; he's, like, Sicilian. He totally wanted to, like, make me his wife!" Her friend counters, "That guy's not Sicilian. He was adopted; he's from Oklahoma. I saw his ID, and his name's Michael Jackson . . . No, really, that's what it said!"

There are many others that blur together. Some sort of restraint pervaded over the whole night, as if they were all going through the motions, doing all this out of custom rather than any true feeling of elation. Grimly pushing through toward dawn.

Outside a gated condo, a girl runs up, followed by a man. "You're my savior! I just wanna go home and sleep. We have to wait for my friend though." With increasing impatience, the two watch as another girl fumbles with the intercom, then goes inside the building. "I'd have been fine clearing out their hall closet and sleeping in it. They made us leave because they wanted to fuck, and now we have to sit out here and wait for HER!" he bitches. Eventually the wayward one returns, and we shove off. The quarreling dies down, replaced by yawns and gentle snores, a night of carousing reducing them all to a trusting childlike state. It's time for bed. For drivers as well as passengers.

The sky is just beginning to lighten when I open the mailbox. A letter from the AARP, complete with member's card, awaits my attention. Had this night really lasted a decade? In any case, it is time to reset the calendar and start the whole damn thing over again . . .

POSTSCRIPT

Many of my cab stories started as short text messages to friends and, later, to acquaintances on Twitter. It became a good way to take notes about what was happening right after it happened.

Some messages, however, didn't warrant any elaboration. Here are the best of those.

"Nobody wants to work, everybody wants money," the old man tells the gas station clerk before reaching his arm into the trash can up to the shoulder to riffle through expired lottery tickets.

A fat man with pants down to ankles urinates behind an open car door in the median of the Southbound Kennedy as rush-hour traffic rolls by.

A shirtless, barefoot, potbellied gentleman is ambling eastbound on Chicago Avenue. Watch out River North, here he comes!

A woman weaves wildly in and out of traffic. The cat on her lap has two paws on the wheel. Not certain who's steering.

Men wearing sandwich boards advertising "40% OFF MEN'S SUITS" patrol Michigan Avenue like medieval penitents in the town square.

A drunk girl staggers across the street and asks to be taken to the Hotel Allegory.

An angry man in a white van does a violent masturbation panto-
mime in order to encourage traffic to move faster, allowing him to
make a turn.

A crude handwritten sign on Archer tempts passersby with "50 YEARS
OF QUALITY SAUSAGE."

Currently tailing a Chicago police cruiser with an "I ♥ SHEMALES"
sticker proudly displayed.

"That was brutal," I say—the rain had made a $10 ride cost $16.
"That's all right," she says. "I'm wearing sweatpants and high heels,
so who am I to judge?"

A little boy asks, "Isn't Chinatown just a town in China?" and his dad is completely flummoxed.

As we pass Oz Park, one oaf points and says, "Got a blow job on that slide seventeen years ago!" His buddy asks me, "Is this *Taxicab Confections*?"

A man walks up Grand Avenue carrying a 24-pack of Keystone Light and a tire; some people just know how to party.

"If you ever call me again, I will personally kill myself because of you, Richard," she said, then went back to blowing smoke out the window.

"We were only friends when she was into irony . . ."

"Go to the flea market? It's where I got my start, worth half a mil six months after I got here," he said, then wandered away without paying for the cab.

"That's the thing, Kev. When I'm hammered, I can't even tell if the girl is hot."

I'm arguing routes with a man who has missed his mouth with most of the nachos he is attempting to consume.

Behind a Volvo with piece of paper taped to the windshield saying, "R.I.P. Dad 12/20/09," in a child's scrawl along with a sketch of the sun.

A girl whacks her eye with the corner of the cab door but continues on to the bar despite a cut and swelling. "They have ice there," she says.

Now comes one of my favorite hours of the night—when drunks begin to discuss whether and to what extent they are indeed drunk.

"I'm SO EXCITED, I wanted to fake-tan but I didn't . . ."

Past Western, an empty shopping cart crosses 95th Street seemingly under its own steam, narrowly missing my cab before continuing on.

ACKNOWLEDGMENTS

This book would not have been possible without two guys' enthusiasm for my work: Levi Stahl of the University of Chicago Press and Whet Moser formerly of the *Chicago Reader*. Great thanks to both for making the initial push.

Bill Savage took his red pen to several early drafts, and by the fall of 2010 we more or less had a book. I must also thank him for inviting me to ball games even if he is a Cubs fan.

Robert Devens, Anne Goldberg, Erin DeWitt, Lindsay Dawson, Elizabeth Fischer, Isaac Tobin, and everyone else at University of Chicago Press who patiently guided this nonwriter through the publishing process.

Shay DeGrandis read early chapters and made suggestions that changed the way I thought about how to organize this book. She also made many wonderful meals and gave me a place to sit quietly and put this book together.

My parents, Alex and Nora Samarov, bought me a critical month of freedom from cab driving to finish this project. No one could wish for a more supportive family (even in times when I haven't necessarily deserved it).

I thank the publications that ran stories from *Hack*: the *Chicago Reader*, *CellStories*, *Chicago Dispatcher*, and the *Printed Blog*.

Many in the Chicago media have been very generous to me: Nick Digilio of WGN Radio 720 AM, *Gapers Block*, *Windy Citizen*, *Chicagoist*, as well as all the other newspapers, journals, blogs, websites, and e-zines that mentioned my work over the years.

Lastly, a qualified thanks to the Yellow, Checker, American United, and Carriage Cab companies of Chicago, Illinois, for renting me the vehicles that provided the setting for these stories.

Acknowledgments